Democracy:
The Long Revolution

Democracy:
The Long Revolution

Edited by
David Powell and Tom Hickey

with contributions by
Colin Richmond; William Lamont; John Newsinger;
John Charlton; David Powell; Paddy Maguire;
Gill Scott; Tony Benn; Tom Hickey

continuum

Continuum UK
The Tower Building
11 York Road
London SE1 7NX

Continuum US
80 Maiden Lane
Suite 704
New York, NY 10038

www.continuumbooks.com

First published 2007

British Library Cataloguing-in-Publication Data
A catalogue record for this book is available from the British Library.

ISBN 08264 86762

Typeset by YHT Ltd, London
Printed and bound by MPG Books Ltd, Bodmin, Cornwall

Contents

Foreword   vii
    Michael Mansfield, QC

Introduction: Indefinite Deferment – 'Two Cheers for Democracy'   1
    David Powell and Tom Hickey

1   **Patience, Humility, Reticence – Hijacked Virtues**   14
    Colin Richmond

2   **The English Civil War and the Putney Debates**   38
    William Lamont

3   **Colonial Wars and Liberal Imperialism: a History of Parliamentary Failure**   57
    John Newsinger

4   **Chartism – a Movement Before its Time**   82
    John Charlton

5   **Labourism – What's Left?**   96
    David Powell

6   **Labour and the New Social Order**   115
    Paddy Maguire

7   **A Protracted Arc: Sex, Gender and Sexuality – Emancipation and Liberation**   131
    Gill Scott

8   **Democracy – the Long Revolution**   150
    Tony Benn in conversation with David Powell

9   **Globalization, Exclusion and the Future of Democracy**   175
    Tom Hickey

Further reading   195

About the contributors   199

Index   203

The Democratic revolution commands our political attention. Here the conflicts are most explicit, and the question of power involved makes it very uneven and confused. Yet in any general view it is impossible to mistake the rising determination, almost everywhere, that people should govern themselves, and make their own decision, without concession of this right to any other group, nationality or class ... Whether in popular revolution, in the liberation movements of colonial peoples, or in the extension of parliamentary suffrage, the same basic demand is evident. Yet the demand has been and is being the very powerfully resisted, not only by the weight of other traditions but by violence and fraud. If we take the criterion that people should govern themselves it is evident that the democratic revolution is at an early stage.

Raymond Williams
The Long Revolution, 1961

Foreword

This is history with meaning, passion and purpose. A broad and truly remarkable canvas is painted with perspectives that put current events into stark relief. Everyone who treasures the fundamental freedoms fought for, and forged, over the last millennium, will find these essays refreshing, revitalizing, and rivetingly informative. Above all, they have a compelling relevance to the challenges facing all of us at this time.

The United Kingdom is currently engaged in a war which is both morally and legally without justification. Having begun with one deceit – W.M.D. – it continues with another, the installation of 'democracy'. How defined? In whose name? On what terms? For whose benefit?

The term 'democracy' has become steadily degraded and usurped over the last century by both totalitarian and non-totalitarian regimes in order to lend a cloak of respectability to what is otherwise naked power-brokering. In Iraq it is a thinly veiled exercise in replacing one form of oppression (political) with another (economic).

At the same time as all of this, and almost in the same breath, the powers allegedly importing democracy in Iraq reject the product of democratic elections elsewhere when they regard the result as unacceptable – namely Palestine. A not dissimilar position was adopted by the British Government in relation to Sinn Fein candidates elected in Northern Ireland.

On the domestic front however, there is a deeper and more far-reaching malaise, namely democratic bankruptcy. We have a system that spawns a Government with one of the lowest proportions of popular vote in Europe. In the last election, Labour won a majority of 67 with only 35% of the votes cast and the support of just 22% of the electorate. As a result, we have a centrist, autocratic and pre-sidential-style of government, unwilling to heed the swathes of popular opposition (especially to the war). As Tony Benn points out in Chapter 8, this fulfils Lord Hailsham's prediction of an 'elective dictatorship'. No wonder there are generations of young people who feel excluded and alienated from the political process. This was notably revealed in Baroness Kennedy's independent inquiry into Britain's democracy for the Joseph Rowntree Reform Trust in 2006. No wonder is it that even the Archbishop of Canterbury is driven to deliver a devastating critique of the Blair years on the basis that they have undermined and damaged democracy (University sermon at St Benet's Church, Cambridge. April 2004).

In this context therefore, this book is a voyage of rediscovery touching on the many brave souls who have joined the struggle for the long revolution. What is striking, whether one starts with the Anglo-Saxons or the Levellers and Diggers or the Chartists, or, more recently, the early Labour Party itself, is that the only real progress has been made by the activities of extra-parliamentary groupings. At p. 149, in the chapter by Gill Scott on the Women's Movement, she poses this question: 'Wherein therefore does democracy reside?' Her answer follows swiftly: 'In the case of the legislative gains secured in women's favour, it would be hard not to conclude that, in the absence of extra-parliamentary initiatives – agitation, organisation, demonstration – there would have been anything more than pious parliamentary eloquence from the legislature and its executive incumbents.' The struggle, therefore, is far from over and requires the continued participation – however small – of everyone who cares.

On a personal note, the voyage has been a poignant one for me. I live near the site of the Putney debates; A.D. Lindsay, who wrote *The Modern Democratic State*, was the inspiration for the new university of Keele that I attended in the 1960s; I am patron of the Tom Paine Project centred in Lewes and, finally, I am privileged to count Tony Benn as a brother-in-arms.

Michael Mansfield QC
February 2007

Indefinite Deferment – 'Two Cheers for Democracy'

David Powell and Tom Hickey

Six decades have passed since E. M. Forster published *Two Cheers for Democracy*, a title which captured something of the optimism of the time, the dawn of the so-called Second Elizabethan Age. Even then, however, Forster could only manage two cheers rather than three – the one, as he wrote, because it admits variety, the other because it permits criticism. As for the missing third cheer, he remained notably silent. Why only two cheers for democracy? Why not three, or even four? The question is as valid as the answer is both clear and as relevant today as it was for Forster. While it is plausible to raise two cheers, the third must remain for what has still to be achieved. This is not some temporary reticence while we await some impending final achievement of democracy's full flourishing. It is a semi-permanent condition. Democracy, as we shall see, could be described as the kind of process whose promise must be endlessly deferred. Even when the conditions of its possible attainment have been secured, its continued flourishing will require continual renewal of ingenuity. For its labourers, there is no end to the day; there is no final state of rest; though there is a clear end to be attained in general terms, there is no static practice or institution that will permanently satisfy that end.

Democracy is, of course, an elusive concept, not least when left to the mercy of historians. The problem is compounded at a time when the approach of TV gurus smacks less of academic rigour than the pick-'n'-mix practices of a local superstore: 'The Virgin Queen?

She's in cosmetics – aisle 13 …'; 'Cromwell? Oh, Cromwell. He's been remaindered. Two for the price of one! Sorry, sir, but revolutions have passed their sell-by date'; and 'No, sir, we don't stock dissent.' A parody certainly, but one with a residue of truth. It is as if we are incapable of following the storyline of our own past unless it is provided with an anodyne spin. This is a past that centres, in large part, on the contest for democracy.

So much, of course, is explicable, for once stripped of illusions, history is revealed for what it really is: a highly subversive subject posing dangerous questions about our inheritance, it invites the interrogation of the status of rights and liberties – the bitterly contested and always fragile rights and liberties – that we possess today. An exaggeration? Not so. Orwell was right when he wrote: 'He who controls the past, controls the present', for, with a few notable exceptions, history has been written by the victors, which may do something to explain the populist spin to which so much of history is subjected. Indeed, there is a certain irony in the fact that while Blair and Brown invoke the history of 'Britishness', and the importance of the subject in the curriculum, both tend to minimize their references to the past, and to the role that the socialist movement has played in the pursuit of democracy. History is performatively espoused even as the past is expunged so that the possibility of alternative futures may be erased.

And yet, just occasionally, reality emerges, as when Bertrand Russell wrote: 'Continuity in government represents no real need of national safety but merely a closing up of the ranks of the governing classes against their common enemy: the people.' Russell was writing from experience, his ancestors having bestrode power in Britain for more than four hundred years. But was he right, or merely paranoid? Was there something to his charge that power perpetuates itself, or, always the *agent provocateur,* was he merely being contentious? Only one thing is certain: that it is only as a result of challenging the orthodoxies of power, of Russell's 'continuity of government', that we have secured the democratic rights that we prize today, and for whose future the authors of these essays, in their different ways, are all of them expressing concern.

2

The illusion, homogenized and carefully packaged – history commodified – is that they are God-given, or, rather, the result of the beneficence of his temporal agents, the great and the good. Nothing could be further from the truth. Each has been hard won, and all still remain vulnerable. In fact, that is the story within the story; not a history retailed piecemeal but a story of the pursuit – the long pursuit – of what people came to regard as their democratic rights, changing and evolving over time. Superficially, the history of the realization of these rights may appear haphazard, random events lacking continuity or coherence. So much is inevitable. Many related factors – political, economic, cultural, social, technological – have helped to shape our present. The whole remains consistent, nevertheless. In fact, the continuities are compelling as if, like some restless daemon, the ideal of democracy – 'the password primeval', as the poet Walt Whitman called it – is not to be denied.

In short, Russell was wrong. Since the Barons at Runnymede compelled John to accept that 'No freeman shall be taken or imprisoned, or in any way destroyed, except by the lawful judgement of his peers'; since Rainborough maintained in the aftermath of the Civil War, 'I think it's clear that every man who is to live under government ought first by his own consent to put himself under government'; and since Tom Paine asserted in the *Rights of Man*, 'There never did, there never will, and there never can exist a Parliament, or any description of men, possessed of the right or power of binding and controlling posterity to the end of time', one thing had remained constant. Russell's governing classes have fought a long rearguard action in defence of their privileges. Nevertheless, though they continually closed their ranks against their common enemy, it has been the people who, ultimately, secured their advance.

Not that this is grounds for complacency. Quite the reverse. As Tony Benn notes, what has been so hard won can all-too-easily be lost. Indeed, that is the essence of the long revolution waged in pursuit of our rights and liberties, of action and reaction locked in a seemingly timeless contest that demarks the boundaries of power. It is this which clearly provides Benn with his faith in the future – that for all the setbacks – the promises betrayed, the undertakings violated – the forward march of democracy has not been halted; that what was once, and not so distantly, regarded as visionary – the right to free speech and free assembly, the right to the vote and freedom of religion, and the right to equality before the law – has been secured.

That, however, is to begin at the end, which is always a dangerous pastime. Though the future is ineluctably shaped by the past, it is not determined by it, or rendered predictable. The problem as far as *The Long Revolution* is concerned is to determine where, exactly, that past begins. What triggered the first, inchoate demands for that 'charming form of government, democracy', which the British have come to regard as their patrimony, and what were the forces and factors which shaped them? In short, what were the primal roots of British democracy? The objective of this book is to trace those origins, and to follow the evolution of those rights and liberties that are so often taken for granted. As such, it makes no pretence of being comprehensive. The nine chapters provide no more than a brief introduction to their subjects, insights into those moments in time when it did, indeed, seem as if the world was being turned upside down.

In the opening chapter, Colin Richmond traces the roots of the powerfully held belief in the rights of the 'freeborn Englishman' from Anglo-Saxon through to Tudor times, which dovetails, exactly, with the provocative introduction to William Lamont's Chapter 2 on the origins of the English Civil War. The majority of Lamont's chapter, however, is devoted to the curious history of the Putney Debates. These arguments racked the Commonwealth, providing, as they did, the point and counterpoint of a seminal dispute as to where constitutional power should lie. In Chapter 4, John Charlton limns in the background, then tracks the rise and fall of the Chartist movement, termed by Carlyle 'The condition-of-England Question', a subject which finds its mirror image in John Newsinger's chapter on Britain's colonial ventures in the nineteenth century (Chapter 3).

The bitter, and seemingly timeless, contest for women's rights, political and economic, forms the basis of Gill Scott's Chapter 7, followed by David Powell's brief history of the formation, and subsequent divisions that racked the Labour party (Chapter 5). In his study of 'Labour and the New Social Order' (Chapter 6), Paddy Maguire takes up the history of the Party post-1945 which, in turn, provides the basis for Tony Benn's critique of New Labour (Chapter 8). Finally, Tom Hickey raises some questions about the prospects for democracy in a global environment (Chapter 9).

Such a fragmented approach, concentrating, as it does, on specific periods and events, may appear to lack continuity, but the contest for democracy has never been a steady state affair. Nonetheless, these moments of the past played a significant role in shaping what had yet to come. If the radicals of the Civil War were quick to make a bogey of the Norman Yoke, radicals, such as Laski and Tawney, were just as quick to call up Tom Paine's *Rights of Man* in their critique of twentieth-century society. Thus the apparent lack of continuity is deceptive, for, while each of the present chapters is freestanding, all share a common root in their pursuit of raising a third cheer for democracy. For that cheer to ring out, however, democrats must come to terms with the silences that attend 'democracy' as a catch-all term – one that occludes the divisions of its history rather than revealing them.

The dominant rhetorical position today is one that celebrates democracy as the requisite accompaniment of a liberal capitalist order in which private property is inviolate, and in which personal liberty from the attentions of the state is secured. Democracy is presented as the enemy of collectivist tyranny, and is equated with representative parliamentary government. Democracy and liberalism are presented as marching hand in hand through history. The long history of the struggle for its attainment is thus collapsed into the fight for the vote, for universal suffrage. This is a selective and misleading story. It does not tell us that democracy and liberalism were not always companions or allies; it does not tell us what once it was that first brought them together, what then divided them, and how and why they were brought together again in the twentieth century. It does not tell us about how struggles for democracy in the past were certainly about political power, and which kinds of people were to control it, but that they were not *only* about that. They were also about wealth and wellbeing, and who should have the right to material security and to a dignified life. The dominant narrative of democracy does not tell us that most of those engaged in yesterday's militant fights for democracy were not only, or even chiefly, concerned about electoral processes but about what the substantive consequences would be for the distribution of wealth, for access to resources, and for an altered position in the world. The fight for universal suffrage was a key element of this struggle but it was not all.

As is clear from a consideration of the English Civil War, the coalition of forces opposed to the old order embraced groups which shared a common enemy in the power of the Crown but who shared little else. If Cromwell and Ireton were determined to defend their interests against the presumptions of the King, even to the point of regicide, it is not a project they could have envisaged, much less accomplished, without 'the middling sort' – the craftsmen and traders, and their apprentices and employees, who constituted the engine of change against the timidity of the reformers. If the latter were more fearful of civil war than of surrender, then the former put iron in the soul of the revolution that the Civil War constituted. The New Model Army, moreover, depended, in part, on the mobilization of those who would become Levellers and Diggers. These then the radical democrats and egalitarians, respectively, who would come to ask what the battle was for unless to secure their interests and a better world, both of which movements Cromwell would suppress, in recognition of the incompatible class interests represented by their ideas and stations, and his own.

This process of coalition-building and subsequent fracturing was not peculiar to the early modern history of English democracy, however. It is a pattern repeated in all of the great revolutionary struggles for democracy against tyranny. We can list them: the American War for Independence of 1776; the French Revolution of 1789; the San Domingue Revolution of slaves in 1792; the Revolutions of 1848; the 1917 revolutions, first against Tsarism and then against capitalism in Russia; the revolutions against Stalinism in Eastern Europe from 1989; the protracted struggle against Apartheid in South Africa; and the overthrow of the Suharto dictatorship in Indonesia in 1998. All have united liberals with those aspiring to a more equal and to a more malleable world in the face of their common enemy. In all cases, however, these coalitions quickly came apart after their immediate victories had been achieved. While liberals who were struggling for democracy only in the form of an electoral political process considered their aims to have been accomplished with the overthrow of tyranny, the egalitarians had been fighting tyranny both in itself and because they wanted economic and social justice as well. That dual objective is what constituted their motivation; its only partial deliverance was then the source of their disappointment, their disillusionment and their disorganization.

This was the case with the Jacobin radicals who would not countenance the aspirations of the *sans coulottes*, which constituency constituted their social base. The suppression and dissolution of the latter as an effective force paved the way for the counter-revolution against radicalism. It was the case in San Domingue, where the great leader of the slave revolution, Toussaint L'Ouverture, dissipated his support amongst the liberated slaves by imposing a labour discipline in the interests of modernization and economic development, and thus prepared his own defeat at the hands of a Napoleonic invasion intent on the restoration of slavery. It was the case in Eastern Europe where the 'self-limiting revolutions' of Solidarnosz in Poland, and its counterparts in Czechoslovakia and elsewhere, ushered in a transformation of Stalinist functionaries and bureaucrats into a private capital-owning and managing bourgeoisie, and thereby demoralized their core supporters. In South Africa, the insistence of the African National Congress, and the South African Communist Party, that the struggle was only about democracy in the narrow sense, with the struggle for social justice indefinitely delayed, heralded the eventual embrace of neo-liberal globalization with all of its attendant consequences for the jobless, for the landless and for the poor.

These were not failures of recognition. It is unlikely that most democrats actively engaged in these struggles were unable to distinguish between democracy as a political process, and democracy as a social and an economic objective. If you risk life and limb, you tend to some idea of the stakes – you know your ambition yet you may not necessarily be able to name it in terms that can map a feasible future. That has not always been the case.

The year 1848 was pivotal in this regard for both wings of the democratic movement: liberals and radicals. The revolutions of that year had a clarifying effect. After 1848, liberals were less concerned with opposition to the tyranny of monarchs and the residual power of the nobility in Europe, and increasingly concerned about the threat from the radical wing of the movement. From the mid-nineteenth century, 'democracy' had become the rallying cry of those opposed to the inequities of the industrial capitalist order, and its dehumanizing forms of urbanization. There emerged the powerful argument from the left, articulating the periodic dissatisfactions of democratic promise over two centuries, that there could be no genuine political democracy without social and economic equality. The struggle was not just about political processes; it was centrally about the outcome in respect of an equal distribution of economic power and influence. What was the value of equal political votes in periodic elections if some could vote with their wallets to influence major decisions on a daily basis? What value has political democracy when capital rules *de facto*? What was required was a thoroughgoing democracy that would address the social question – a Social Democracy.

The refrain of the Levellers and of the Diggers echoed down two centuries, but was now voiced in different circumstances. No longer the utopian hope of the millenarian dispossessed and impoverished, as in the 1640s in England, it was now the chant of a substantial, geographically concentrated and urbanized working class that was increasingly organized in trade unions, and represented by political parties. Once the subordinate, if crucial, allies of the liberal wing of democracy, the lower orders had now become a threat to the very freedom of capital to invest and to accumulate that liberal ideology had been elaborated to justify and to legitimate. The response of liberals, gradually but distinctively, was not just a combination of governmental repression or concession (depending on the balance of forces) but a gradual conceptual distancing of liberalism from democracy. Or rather, a not so subtle redefinition of 'democracy' to exclude its social element, and thus to focus exclusively on democracy only as a desirable process of government formation. Thus, an increasingly exclusive concentration on the project as a formal process so as to evacuate it of its substantive content.

But circumstances dictate strategy. It was never desirable for liberalism to abandon the field, to yield up any notion of democracy as incompatible with its individualism and with private accumulation. If the accommodation of Social Democracy with capitalism on continental Europe and in the UK during the inter-war years began the shift of circumstances, the consequences of first the victory and then the defeat of Fascism completed it. The Cold War was a new terrain in which the slogan of democracy could again be wielded as a weapon by liberalism. Now Social Democracy followed the logic of its accommodation, with the greatest alacrity in Britain, as Paddy Maguire's essay demonstrates. If the Fabian socialism of Beatrice and Sidney Webb in the 1920s and 1930s had always been patronizing and condescending to a working population that had to be rescued from its own occasional bouts of radical excess, Labour's leadership could recognize a recalcitrant enemy when it encountered one. Now unexpectedly at the helm of the ship of state after the war, it would not be blown off course by ambitions that it had not sanctioned.

To where could exasperated democrats turn in these circumstances in the face of an overbearing Labour Government? Not to the Communist Parties of the West, seen, as they increasingly were, as the foreign policy tools of a regime which constituted the antithesis of both substantive and procedural democracy. This was the opportunity to collapse any distinction between representative assemblies and universal adult suffrage, on the one hand, and the project of democratization, on the other. This was the epoch in which that doyenne of intellectual anti-communism, Isaiah Berlin, could mischievously refract a Kantian distinction into the difference between 'positive' and 'negative' freedom. Only the latter, i.e. freedom from constraint (governmental constraint, naturally), was a genuine freedom. The former, a freedom of those who have been enabled to act through the provision of the necessary resources (i.e. the socialist project of achieving equitable outcomes) could only be attained at the cost of a tyrannical social order. Stalinism was his implicit evidential proof of the thesis.

So ubiquitous did this collapse of democracy into representative process become that radical democrats found themselves marginalized, excoriated and lampooned. If this was an epoch in which socialism could be reduced by Anthony Crosland to 'what Labour Governments do' then democracy was equally prone to glib reduction: it was the type of political system that 'we' happen to have here and now. Historically and theoretically risible as an argument, it nevertheless established itself as popular common sense. In such a political climate, the concept of democracy had truly been eviscerated. Worse, much worse, was to follow.

If democracy was once the siren cry to wed liberals and radicals in a common struggle against the old feudal order, only to be reinterpreted as an impoverished cousin of liberalism when radicalism threatened the rights of property, it was to have yet a new life at the end of the twentieth century. The 1980s witnessed the final exhaustion of the Social Democratic and Labourist projects, most sharply signalled by the policy vicissitudes of the French Socialist Party under François Mitterrand. The manipulation of electoral rules to avoid defeat by giving an opening to the fascist Front Nationale of Le Pen, was perhaps the most craven act of parliamentary careerism.

With Stalinist societies having imploded, and Social Democratic tinkering no longer possessing appeal, the entrenched conservative governments of Margaret Thatcher, Helmut Kohl and Ronald Reagan could present themselves as the exemplars of the only model of democratic representation available. They could so do even as their policies systematically eroded the elements of substantive democracy that post-war welfare Keynesianism had achieved. Now 'democracy' could be brandished as a weapon against enemy regimes: liberalize your economies, and provide access for our investments, or we will fund a domestic movement amongst your population that will agitate for democracy in our style, and destabilize your society in our interests. This was a new dispensation, and one that would later be refined first by the Clinton–Blair axis in the form of 'humanitarian war' in defence of universal human rights, and in defiance of international law. Later, the project would be further advanced by the Bush–Blair axis in the form of 'democratic imperialism' – you will have democracy, and you will have it in the form that we have managed to confect, and by which we have managed to limit its radicalism here. Thus, from 'B-52 liberals' to exporters of self-determination at the point of a bayonet, and the behest of an Apache helicopter.

This is, of course, a more complex history than democracy is usually allowed. It is also a more contested history. There is not one democracy but many. Or, at least, there are two: a liberal democracy concerned purely with political processes, and a substantive and socialist democracy concerned with outcomes and effects. The latter's concern is for outcomes (for justice and equality) not at the expense of personal freedoms and political rights but as the objectives for which these democratic processes are the required means. Those are the lessons of the partial achievements and manifest limitations of the different moments addressed by the essays in this volume. The sharpest lesson that this history teaches, however, and the most poignant given the loss of collective memory about these struggles, is that, far from being its companion, liberalism and democracy have been incompatible political projects since the middle of the nineteenth century.

In opening this book, we suggested that democracy was and is an 'unfinished project'. One of the difficulties of such a formulation is that it leaves the project essentially indeterminate. Given the core argument of this essay, however, that democracy is unavoidably imbricated in the struggle for equality and justice, that is clearly not our intent. What we intend rather is the view that the nature of the struggle for a fair and equitable society changes over time. This struggle once required the recognition that liberation from oppression and exploitation could not be attained in England without the simultaneous liberation of those in India or Ireland

11

from British colonialism. Today, in altered circumstances, it means recognizing that the struggle for liberation and dignity at home requires a challenge to the notions of citizenship and 'belonging' that are being constructed for us. It also requires us to submit to critical scrutiny the role of national boundaries in determining our identities, and the determination of those with whom we can identify. We can no longer struggle for liberation and wellbeing within the parameters of a nation or a regional bloc. That would be to turn a Nelson's eye to the squalor, destitution and indignity of perhaps 80 per cent of humanity, most of whom happen to live in Africa, Asia and Latin America. Such a discriminating eye could only be a racial one. Our propensity to empathize, and consequent capacity to sympathize (our 'moral sympathy', to use Adam Smith's formulation) would not allow us to tolerate such conditions to be suffered by others at 'home'. That is a practice and an attitude utterly incompatible with any conceivably defensible notion of democracy.

If the battle remains one of human liberation, as it does, then today the terrain on which it is fought has shifted, and so too the precise nature of the engagements. That the achievement of the aim is indefinitely deferred as circumstances change does not mean that it can never be attained in principle. That would be a counsel of despair. That democracy is an 'unfinished project' does not mean that it is an 'unfinishable project', even if, like any human practice, it will always require continual renewal. Indefinite deferral, moreover, is not the same as 'endless deferral'. If, as we have suggested, democracy as an end, as a condition of and for wellbeing and the struggle for its attainment before that moment, is an unavoidable condition of humanity then the end can be reached. Humanity is not trapped as an ineluctably alienated species, possessed of an ambition and a drive that it can never realize. We do not have to live out the agonism of permanent lack, while deluding ourselves as to the practicality of our projects.

Central to these concerns then must be a recognition of democracy not as a set of abstract principles but as the outcome of a general striving by humanity for a better life. It is thus a practical expression of the human condition whose ambition and forms of expression are necessarily historical and context bound. This recognition issues in two conclusions. The first is that democracy emerges not just as a means to the attainment of the good life, which aim was its provocation, but rather, in the recurrence and persistent recurrence of its struggle, seems to be a *necessary* means. It is, in one sense at least, the *only* outcome of rational reflection on the requisite political conditions for improvement with which history has furnished us hitherto. The second conclusion is that the variety of forms which democracy takes are, unavoidably, stamped by the character of the underlying struggles of which it is both expression and means.

Democracy is not simply, or even mainly, a technique for government formation, on the one hand, and consequent social control via the legitimization of political authority, on the other. That may be the dominant mode of its treatment in political science literature, and in the rhetoric of professional politicians and media pundits, but it is not remotely adequate. As one critic has observed, this reduction of it to technical processes constitutes the 'depoliticization' of democracy. By abstracting the idea of it from the historical struggles for its attainment, and hence from the social and material conditions of those contexts, is to misrepresent democracy as a fixed set of institutions and procedures rather than as the dynamic process that it has always been. It is also to displace its core motivation: the popular aspiration for a better future captured in our utopian visions – those 'good' utopias which are not just better than the present state of things but, as developments from the present, are simultaneously feasible. It is to the recuperation of those motivations, aspirations and visions, in other words to the recovery of the original spirit and intent of democracy as a liberating project, that the following chapters are dedicated.

Chapter 1

Patience, Humility, Reticence – Hijacked Virtues

Colin Richmond

There were varieties of freedom in Anglo-Saxon England. This we know from the various penalties imposed on men for criminal violence, these varied according to status. There were slaves who had no value in the eyes of the law, there were prisoners of war, criminals, those born in slavery, and those who enslaved themselves (so to speak) by falling into debt. All other men, though not women, were to a greater or lesser degree free. Those who worked the land, whom for the sake of convenience we call peasants (*paysans:* the people of the *pays* or countryside) were the least 'free', but then the freedom of the small man was invariably circumscribed by economic if not legal circumstance. Most Anglo-Saxon peasants were subsistence farmers, but like all such they need to buy salt and iron, let alone seed corn and small livestock, at a market, so from early days the English economy was as much a market economy as it was a subsistence economy, hence the getting into debt of unthrifty or war-damaged farmers. But legally the obligations to a landlord of the great majority of these small producers (the *ceorls*) were never onerous enough for them to be considered other than freemen. So it was before the Danish and Norman conquests. Warfare on a national scale began the changes that led to the great majority of *ceorls* being transformed into *villeins*, unfreemen. These changes, and such resistance to them as could be (and was) mounted, will form the first part of this essay.

Part One

The Danish conquest of the north and east of England and the reconquest of those parts by Alfred and his successors had two important consequences. The first will not detain us long. The Danes who settled in East Anglia, the East Midlands and the East Riding, and the Norwegians who colonized the Isle of Man, northern Lancashire and Cumbria, brought with them a tradition of freedom associated with a way of life that combined farming with trade, pillage and bloody murder. They were in every respect bloody-minded. No one told them what to do.

Where we are concerned, there are two aspects of such an attitude to life which had lasting results. First, where the Danes and Norwegians settled they did so as free farmers. There may not have been many of them, but they brought to Eastern and North Western England a reinforcement to the freedom of the English *ceorls* who had lived there. The free peasantry of the Danelaw (as East Anglia and much of midland and eastern England came to be called) and of the lands beyond the Ribble were not all Scandinavians, but it was the Scandinavian concept of freedom that asserted itself there long after the Norman Conquest.

Secondly, those ideas of freedom were embodied in assemblies, like the long-lasting 'parliaments' of Iceland and the Isle of Man. These gatherings at the local level, of freemen of the shire and hundred, were to play a part in the development of the English Parliament itself, a talking shop of the freemen of the whole realm. Before 1066 and for some time afterwards, a freeman was also a nobleman. The Scandinavian warrior-farmer was 'noble' even if he owned little more than a croft and a place on the rower's bench of a longship. In that respect he was not unlike the later Polish gentleman (*szlachta*), who the less wealthy he was the more fiercely independent he became, so much so that the political Polish nation was eventually undermined in the 1790s by his unwillingness to collaborate either with his fellows or the government. This did not happen in England for a whole host of reasons, among them being the fact that the Scandinavian sense of 'freedom at all costs' gave place to something more civilized: mutual cooperation for the sake of public good.

The Scandinavian farm and household economies ran smoothly, allowing the farmer and his sons the time to go abroad and behave badly, because they were slave economies. As in Greece and Rome a handful of men might be free because a multitude of other men and women were not. Such freedom allowed for the cultivation and elaboration of ideas, not least ideas about the state: Platonic, Aristotelian, and at the court of Alfred the Great, Asserian. Thus we arrive at Wessex and the re-conquest of Danish England by the kings of Wessex in the tenth century. Alfred halted the Danish advance just when it seemed that all was lost, drove the Danes out of the West Country, and re-conquered London, England's chief town, though not its capital: that was Winchester because, until 1066, England was very much a 'greater' Wessex. By the second half of the century, the conquest of the Danelaw was complete, the coinage of Edgar and Athelred proudly proclaiming that they ruled 'All England'.

But, and in the context of this essay the 'but' looms very large, military endeavour on such a scale always cost huge sums of money to pay for men, horses, arms and armour. It came, as it invariably comes, from the man in the street, in this case the streets of the villages of Wessex. In order to support a warrior class, the *thegns* who did nothing but fight, *ceorls* had to hand over more of their surplus, little though that surplus might be. If this could not be done in the form of a higher rent, then work on the estates of kings, lords and of *thegns* themselves was demanded so that each estate might produce for a market that was strengthening with each passing year. In modern terminology, a more egalitarian society was being turned into a less egalitarian one. In medieval terms, manors were being created where there were no manors previously, a manor by definition being a landed estate with men who work on it for the benefit of the owner. For the *thegns* of Wessex to be free to fight at a day's notice, to campaign for weeks in Staffordshire or Yorkshire, or to guard the Alfredian fortresses, the *burghs* of old Wessex, the former free farmers of the old Wessex heartland of Dorset, Somerset, Wiltshire, Hampshire, Gloucestershire and Worcestershire, had to have their freedom curtailed. They were attached to a manor, they farmed its arable as well as their own; and became obligated in a number of other restrictive ways to the lord of the manor. They were not yet called *villeins* but that is what they were well on the way to becoming.

In the former Danelaw, especially in its most populated (and most fertile) parts – Norfolk, Suffolk and Lincolnshire – the long arm of Wessex reached but did not so firmly grip. There a 'free peasantry' survived. Many of these freemen, these *sokemen* as they were called (for such a man's *soke,* his jurisdiction as we might think of it, was his own and not someone else's, as it was in Greater Wessex), were in possession of farms of no great size, but these were not incorporated into a manorial system, or if they were, only loosely. Manorialization only came later with the Norman Conquest, and even then it never became what it was in the west. I have mentioned that the east of England was heavily settled: the more fertile the soil, the more people it can bear; the more people on the land, the greater the productivity. To the theme of population growth and the upswing in arable production in medieval England we will return. First, however, the Norman Conquest has to be got out of the way.

That conquest was once thought of as the Norman Yoke. That idea has long been out of academic circulation. What happened was no more than an intensification of the manorialization that had got under way in the tenth century. There were more warriors to be provided for, many of them ruffians and rogues, and foreign ones at that, who imposed themselves on the peasantry and made them work harder for smaller rewards. This happened all over England, but less in the north than in the south, and more in the arable heartland of the Midlands than in the pastoral economies of the borderlands towards Wales and the hill country beyond York. The Normans were, however, in every respect conquerors, and they behaved as such: an alien hand is heavier than that of the native. Or so we are led to believe. Yet, late-Anglo-Saxon government as it is now understood, was not only a highly sophisticated bureaucracy, but also a more powerful compulsive machine than the Anglo-Norman one that succeeded it.

Taxation is the key issue in this respect. From the tenth century the Anglo-Saxon kings had an effective taxation system at their command to provide for an army and a navy that was, arguably, the best in northern Europe. The second Scandinavian conquest of England in the early eleventh century – King Cnut and All That – did not disturb the system: in fact that conquest gets only a passing reference because it disturbed very little. The wages of *thegns*, who were equally at home fighting on land as they were at sea, and on foot or on horseback, were paid out of a tax on land that was collected at manorial centres and derived from the labour of an unfree peasantry and the dues they paid in silver pennies (in lieu of chickens, eggs, bacon etc.).

It was this tax which, having got somewhat fossilized, the Normans sought to bring up to date in a survey of the landed resources of their new, and very rich, kingdom, that has always been known as Domesday Book. And make no mistake about it: England was a *very* rich country. That is why the Normans took a great risk in invading it. As luck would have it, they succeeded. It was rich not only in grain, but in wool, and English wool and English cloth were as famous on the continent as English embroidery. London, Norwich, Lynn, Boston, Gainsborough exported English wool and woollens to all parts of the continent. It was because England was so agriculturally wealthy that the taxation system was worth the Normans' bold attempt to update it. They never actually did: the Domesday Book was a tax register that was never used. Other, less efficient, 'feudal' taxes were imposed. It is these that caused the friction which led to Magna Carta. Let us tackle Magna Carta, therefore, before we return to population growth and the hardest of hard times for the English, no longer the Anglo-Saxon, peasantry.

The demonstration that led to the confrontation between barons and king at Runnymede in 1215 was not a popular one. It was a protest of the privileged. John had been fighting a costly war and to

18

pay for it he had been taxing his vassals beyond their endurance. It was not only their ability to pay the feudal exactions he demanded that was at issue, it was how he had gone about it that they baulked at. The charter of agreement sealed between them at Runnymede, in June 1215, did not prevent civil war.

The King of France invaded England, and John was up against it when he over-indulged for the umpteenth time and failed, for the first time, to get away with it. Nor could the Great Charter (of Liberties) have had much in it for others than a few score of disgruntled barons and their knightly followers, whose appearance in arms made the barons' attendance at Runnymede militarily, and therefore politically, possible, had the social diversity of English society not made them scratch their heads over how to ensure the application of those liberties to all who socially and politically mattered. For it was not only barons and knights who mattered in thirteenth-century England. It was not so much the social diversity that was unusual, it was having to come up with words to describe the men who comprised English society (and mattered) that was difficult. It did not often happen. On a nation-wide scale it had not happened until now.

To cut a complicated story short, the only term the drafters could come up with that covered every male that counted in England was freeman (*libero homo*). It was this which made the Great Charter significant for subsequent generations. It was Great, by the by, because it was long. There were 63 clauses, some of them as specific as that which promised the removal of fish weirs from the Thames, or those in which John promised to expel 'foreigners', that is those non-Englishmen whom he had employed as castellans and soldiers; clauses in which we might wish to detect an English chauvinism that has lasted to this day. It is, however, the more general clauses that concern us. Some of them were vague enough to be representative of little except aspiration; the very first, for example: 'that the English church shall be free', or the one which stated: 'To no one will we sell, to no one will we deny or delay right or justice.' But others, especially those protecting the means of livelihood of freemen, granting them freedom from arbitrary arrest and imprisonment, and guaranteeing their property from unlawful sequestration, these, however much they might be broken in practice, survived as markers for critics of overbearing governments in every succeeding epoch. The Great Charter was never rescinded. It was applied to, and cited by all and sundry over the following centuries, medieval and modern.

Who exactly was a freeman was already a matter for the new Common Law courts, which had firmly taken root less than a generation previously. Peasants brought cases against lords who sought to impose or increase their rent and labour obligations. They invariably lost, lawyers and judges being themselves landlords who had no wish to see their own peasants escape into freedom or recover the freedom their fathers and grandfathers had once had. The way to freedom for the peasant did not lie through the courts, it lay in the uncultivated land on the margin of manors and in those counties, Derbyshire and Staffordshire for instance, hitherto on the edge of arable agriculture. Landlords offered free and easy terms to colonists, a shilling an acre rent and no strings attached. These were free peasants. They would count as freemen, however humble and obscure, if and when freedom became an issue.

But such folk were not in the minds of the royal officials and baronial agents who wrangled over the clauses of the Great Charter. It was the men who were not knights, that is, armoured soldiers on horseback, who played just as big a role in civil society that mattered to them: the university-trained clerks who wrote the copies of the Great Charter that were despatched around the kingdom; the judges and lawyers at the king's elbow; the merchants and businessmen of London and other rapidly expanding cities of the kingdom, the craftsmen and shopkeepers of the market towns that were springing up everywhere, in what we must call a developing society, some of them out of nothing whatsoever, like Stratford-on-Avon, successfully floated by the Bishop of Worcester with an eye for profit on a rural manor of no great consequence. Above all there were those landowners who rode horses but never put on armour, those we want (anachronistically) to call gentlemen, perhaps even country gentlemen. The term 'gentlemen' was not available for discussion in

1215. Something else had to serve. Hence freeman, and thus into that catch-all category all sorts of politically insignificant men were included. Many of them would acquire political significance in later centuries when politics came to mean parliament, above all the Commons in Parliament.

The meetings at Runnymede in June, 1215, were called a parliament, the old 1960s term 'talk in' best describing what the word parliament meant in the century of its origin. The crux of the discussions at Runnymede was consultation: a lord had every right to ask for the aid of his vassals, but how much aid, and in what form might he reasonably demand it? Not to threaten the very means of existence of a freeman was how one of the more famous clauses put it. There was plenty to discuss in so broad a definition. Moreover, did not vassals have a say in the matter? They might be obliged to give service, military or monetary, but should they not have a say about how much? The king resisted. No government relishes being questioned as to the necessity of its actions, and once discussion is admitted all sorts of questions might be asked, as they were in 1215. Was the war really necessary, for example? Was it in their interest, or only in the interest of their lord?

John had to give way on the matter of consultation. A king, it was reluctantly admitted by those in government, was not a tyrant. Like any other good lord, if he went to war, embarked on a crusade, or sought to bring the Welsh, Irish and Scots to heel, he ought to ask the advice of his vassals on such matters, especially when it came to financing such enterprises. And who were the vassals of a King of England? Why, every freeman of his realm. Thus, parliament had its origins at Runnymede. Between that parliament and the Long Parliament of 1642 there would run a twisted path, but path it was. Charles I attempting to act the tyrant suffered similar indignities to those imposed on King John who, had he lived longer, might well have lost his head in a civil war that went against him.

This is not a history of parliament. Nevertheless, what happened to parliament in the medieval centuries needs to be outlined at this point, as English freedom is often equated with the English parliament, as it was in 1642, and rightly so. The gist of the matter, where freedom and ultimately democracy is concerned, is the Commons and taxation. First the lords of parliament, as the peerage of England came to be defined as those who received a named summons to consult with the king's government, and afterwards what we know as the House of Commons, whose members were elected, asserted their right to be told why the government needed to tap into the wealth of the rest of the nation, rather than rely on its own resources, and to be informed how much was required.

Essentially, by the 1340s, and by 1376 at the latest, it was the Commons who were crucial to the advertisement, consultation and discussion. The lords were compliant, if only because they knew it was the distinguished lawyers, businessmen and country gentlemen who sat in the Commons who would ask the more searching questions, for they were better informed, more articulate, and less committed to a royal government they might serve, or fight for, but had not been made noble by.

Above all it was the lawyers among the knights of the shire, elected in the county court, and among the members elected by the boroughs, who came to dominate proceedings in the Commons. About a third of the Commons of 1422 came from the legal profession, and that proportion or, some would say, disproportion, grew larger thereafter. It was in the Commons that the critics of government were to be found. It was a situation that did not last. By the second half of the fifteenth century, government had learned how to 'manage' the House of Commons.

Early Tudor parliaments were docile by comparison with those of the late fourteenth and early fifteenth centuries, and Elizabeth became an expert 'manager' of her parliaments. The early Stuarts were incapable of managing anything, least of all a House of Commons sure of its own powers. Those powers are the ones we have outlined above. It is true that they were not much in evidence for close on two centuries, yet they had neither been forgotten nor had they been overridden, as they had been in the case of the Estates General in France, and therefore were there to be invoked when the occasion required it.

A last word about parliament. Elections have been mentioned.

Who qualified to attend elections of the knights of the shire? Who elected borough representatives? Why, freemen of course. So many gentlemen, yeomen, and even husbandmen turned up at fifteenth-century shire elections that the franchise had to be restricted to the better off among them. In the boroughs, the status of freemen became the preserve, if at one time it had not been, of a handful of oligarchs. That is how the elections of lawyers and gentlemen, whom the oligarchs thought would better benefit the town than one of their own, were later 'fixed'. At elections in the shire court, it is true that the bigwigs of the county (the *buzones* as they were known in the thirteenth century) more often than not got the two members they wanted elected, but by no means on every occasion. Moreover, the principle of what we would call 'free' elections persisted in the public mind, and that persistence was crucial to the survival of democracy in England.

But who were these gentlemen, yeomen and husbandmen of fifteenth-century rural England? How was it that they emerged from the peasantry of previous centuries? Here we return to population growth and economic development, the first of which was brutally halted by the Black Death of 1348, the second being diverted into new channels by it. With this brief account, Part One will be concluded.

Of course the tillers of the soil of the thirteenth century were as varied in resources and fortune as those above them in the social hierarchy. One peasant was not like another. It is true, nonetheless, that the unprecedented growth in population of the twelfth and thirteenth centuries was nothing short of disastrous for the great majority of them. That the economy of England in this period was a relatively sophisticated market economy did not help them. On the contrary, as subsistence farmers they were at a grave disadvantage, having little, and increasingly less and less, to sell. Moreover, having little to sell, they had to sell it disadvantageously, when rents were due and grain prices low. If it has not been said already, let it be recalled that every peasant, whether he was free or unfree, was a tenant farmer.

Landlords, despite the technicalities of feudal land law, were as good as landowners. They certainly behaved as such. They were advantageously placed both in terms of the market, and in terms of capital accumulation, and in terms of their own tenant farmers, whose labour they were in a favourable position either to exact in full, or to take a money equivalent. With the latter they could hire increasingly cheap labour from impoverished smallholders and the landless, a group waxing larger year by year as the population of England climbed to six or seven million by 1300. That was a million or more too many for the land to carry comfortably. By that date in a bad year the poorest were starving to death, in the famine years of 1315–17 in their thousands, possibly in their hundreds of thousands

In such conditions, conditions applicable to the contemporary Third World, freedom of any real kind disintegrated and then disappeared. It was a tough cultivator who accumulated other men's half- and quarter-acres, married a village widow, and becoming the lord's reeve, fiddled bills and receipts to 'disappear' a pig or two of his employer's, abused his position to use the lord's oxen for ploughing his own strips in the open fields, and to see that those strips were among the first to be harvested. Such men there were, we might call them the husbandmen of Old England, which is what, by the end of the fourteenth century, they had become, men such as Clement Paston of Norfolk who sent his son to school to become a lawyer, barrister and, crowning achievement this for the son of an erstwhile peasant, Judge of the Court of Common Pleas.

It was not only the small men who went to the wall. Smallholders were often obliged to sell out to greater ones, earls and barons, bishops and abbots, the leaders in the law and government. It is no wonder, then, that the century between 1250 and 1350 was one of social resentment and political bitterness. As Marc Bloch wrote in his classic *French Rural Society* it was a society in which strikes by tenant farmers, obliged to live on less and work longer hours for a master, was endemic. These refusals to work are to be found in the manorial records of southern and midland England, and became increasingly frequent and ever more acrimonious as the thirteenth century gave way to the fourteenth. They were the chief form of resistance to lordly power, that is if we discount the pilfering of grain, chickens and eggs from the lord's barns, which was a fact of manorial life, and the so-called poaching of the rabbits from *his* warren, the deer from *his* woods, and the fish and eel from *his* streams, as all of what once had been open, or common land had been appropriated willy-nilly by the bigwigs of the countryside.

That was resistance too, and it was seen as such. Which is why the foremost literary hero of the time was a poacher: Robin Hood no less. He was also a forester, and a yeoman forester at that. Which brings us not only to the yeomen of England but also returns us to the matter of freedom in medieval England, and how it was perceived. The tales of Robin Hood, it has to be stressed, while not being written down until the fifteenth century, were circulating, and widely, before the Black Death of 1348. Those tales will take a few paragraphs, the last of the first part of this chapter.

Robin Hood was a special sort of yeoman. He was not the sort of Yeoman of England who will occupy us in the second part of this essay. He was not, in other words, a prosperous tenant farmer who rented three or four, or five hundred acres or more from a landlord who was forced by circumstances we shall describe in the second part to lower rents to rock-bottom levels. On those broad acres yeomen farmers ran sheep for mutton as well as wool, fattened beef cattle for the London and export markets, and grew a variety of grain crops – certainly not the sort that produced the diet of porridge his peasant predecessors had lived on a hundred years before, unless they were poachers, that is.

Robin Hood was not tied down like that. He lived in the forest, or rather 'the forest' for that fictional place, somewhere north of Nottingham, across the real administrative divide between North and South, the River Trent, was where freedom might be experienced to its utmost, a Never-Never Land composed of mistaken memories of uncolonized woodland and of kings who, if they only knew what their corrupt sheriffs and castellans were up to, would dismiss them out of hand. Abbots and monks, it should be noted, were pretty universally loathed by all right-thinking men and women, and could be robbed without the least hesitation. Impoverished knights, in debt to grasping abbots, were, on the other hand, to be treated gently, for they were the *gentilhommes* of the day after tomorrow.

Robin himself will become a gentleman too, but not until the tales were updated in the sixteenth century. In the times we are writing about he is brave and brutal, not hesitating to lop off heads, for a sword is more his sort of weapon than a staff. He is also on comically equal terms with craftsmen, market-stall holders, cooks, their wives and daughters. Moreover, he treats the king himself as an equal, though the Sheriff of Nottingham he disdains for the blustering knave and blundering fool that he is. Why can he behave like this? For the simple reason that he, too, is a *gentilhomme*, but of the old fashioned kind, a *libero homo* of the old school, never mind that none ever existed. Hope was given to those who listened to these tales, those who having not known what freedom was, were given in those stories a very clear notion of what it was. Freedom persisted in fiction, despite its disappearance in fact.

Part Two

Robin Hood was an outlaw. The meaning of that is clear. He was not only outside the law; his actions show him to have been anti-law, any law save that issuing directly from the King's mouth. That such law giving might be qualitatively different was, alas, a romantic notion. It was a commonplace of peasant society that there was nothing but grief for anyone who found himself in a law court, whether as defendant, plaintiff, juror, or bondsman. You would, the saying went, always come out the poorer.

There is not the least doubt that lawyers, and those who made a living from the law, were detested, and many such persons were victims of the angry rebels of 1381. The famous uprising has acquired a meaning far beyond, and probably far other than the meaning it had in 1381. To discover what it was, the changes engendered by the Black Death have to be considered. The Peasants' Revolt may have been triggered by the Poll Tax, but it was much more than a demonstration against an inequitable tax. The Revolt is also called 'The Great Revolt of 1381' and justifiably, even if its

London manifestation lasted little more than a fortnight before the agencies of reaction rediscovered their nerve.

The uprising began in late May at Fobbing in Essex with a demonstration of contempt for a local tax official, who was also a JP and a former sheriff. The rising spread quickly, and contact was made with the men of Kent, across the Thames estuary. By mid-June, the joint force was encamped outside London, and on 14 June the young King, Richard II, confronted the rebels at Mile End and granted them their demand for freedom from serfdom. At this point, the men of Essex, well pleased with what had been achieved, quit London. As a result, it was only the men of Kent, led by Wat Tyler, who were at Smithfield on 15 June to present a new series of demands to the King, among them an end to lordship in England, and for rents to be fixed at no more than 4p an acre. If these were not too much for those present with Richard to stomach, they were for the Mayor of London, William Walworth, who struck at an 'insolent' Wat Tyler, probably an agreed signal for those Londoners already in arms to disperse the rebels.

In East Anglia outbreaks of violence continued beyond the middle of June, and everywhere the archives of landowners were confiscated and burned, even at Thaxted where metal workers were prospering and labour services had been commuted 20 years before. Still, would it last? Best to be on the safe side and destroy the records of subservience.

The rebels of 1381 were not to know that villeinage would disappear. The land-owning class had been frightened out of its wits by the rising, and while the government recovered quickly, there was no going back on serfdom, or the wage freeze of the Statute of Labourers of 1351 ('zealously enforced' against employers of labour, though not at all against 'people of higher social rank'), or on the Poll Tax. All commentators are now agreed, however, that the core issue that sparked the revolt was the overwhelming desire of the participants for freedom. So, yet again, the question: What did they mean by freedom? That too seems to be clear: it was to be free of the restrictions on their freedom of action as tenant farmers.

The men who made the revolt in Essex and Kent, and to a lesser extent in Suffolk and Norfolk, were neither landless, nor were they smallholders; they have even been found to be what we are entitled now to call husbandmen, some of them even yeomen, though neither of these terms was yet in common use. They were often the backbone of rural society at village and hundred levels, tithingmen and jurors. Many of them had substantial holdings. They had done well out of the Black Death, leasing vacant holdings, accumulating farms. They were men of enterprise and did not want to be held back.

What did hold them back was that range of manorial obligations that took up their time and money. They were charged for transactions in land and on the sale of livestock; they had to pay a fee if a son wanted to work outside the manor, or a daughter got married; work at the lord's harvest was often still demanded, and money in lieu of other services required. The list might be extended. All such hindrances to prosperity they wanted to be rid of, and wherever they went they burned the manorial documents that recorded them. There was widespread destruction of these much hated records across southern England, often in places the revolt as such never came near. In other words, villeinage was to be abolished.

And it was. It was already disappearing before 1381, and for this state of affairs the Black Death was responsible. The population of England and Wales was certainly halved by the outbreaks of plague that occurred between 1348 and 1370. By 1430 or thereabouts the population had reached its lowest ebb since the eighth or ninth centuries. There may have been no more than 2 or 3 million people scattered across a depopulated countryside. This is the time of deserted villages and abandoned farms. Land became cheap to rent. Labour became dear to employ. Many peasants who had struggled to farm a few acres became agricultural labourers. Others, like many of the rebels of 1381, put strips together, laid some to grass, increased their flock of sheep, and became proto-yeomen, proto-capitalists as some historians are tempted to call them.

Capital could now be accumulated, farmhouses repaired, barns could be built, farm tools bought, better seed purchased. Or it could be, if those outgoings to landlords were abolished, and a straightforward money rent substituted. By the 1370s, the writing was on the wall for what is known as demesne farming – that is a lord farming his non-tenanted land for the market. The price of grain had fallen because there were so many fewer mouths to feed, while the price of hiring labour had risen. More than one manorial account records that expenditure was exceeding revenue, and that demesne farming should cease. This brought more land onto the market, often the best land, and it was demesne leases that were being snapped up by those whom we might be justified as calling the 'bigwigs' of village England.

However, economic and social change never operates without operators. The rebels of 1381 were single-minded and articulate about what they wanted: anything that smacked of unfreedom had to go. And, by 1400 or thereabouts, everything that did had gone. Only pockets of much atrophied villeinage survived, more often than not on great ecclesiastical estates, which were among the slowest to change, for it is a truism that it was the smaller estates, which feeling the pressure earliest and hardest, were the quickest to change. Thus, carrying services on a few of the manors of the Archbishop of Canterbury in Kent were still demanded in the later fifteenth century, and bondmen and women were still to be found on a handful of Duchy of Lancaster properties in the sixteenth century.

Had the Revolt of 1381 not taken place, change would not only have been slower, it might also have been resisted with greater vigour. The Great Revolt scared not only the government; it frightened landowners into compliance with the wishes of their peasant tenants. Economic determinism will not serve. They took the situation into their own hands and made sure their escape would be permanent. Unfortunately, or perhaps inevitably, social and economic freedom meant the end of the English peasantry.

There is no doubt that the fifteenth century was a good time to be alive if you lived and worked in the countryside. This is the century in which lamb, as well as mutton, came onto the market; when the roast beef of old England was eaten by others than lords and ladies, when a wider variety of fruits and vegetables was consumed in greater quantities, when German beer replaced Gascon wine as the

Englishman's tipple, when leather footwear could be afforded by many, and when good English woollen cloth was to be found on most English backs. Indeed, some would say that the average Englishman and his wife ate, drank and dressed better than at any time in the nation's history before 1900. There was, however, a price to pay, there always is when it comes to 'progress' – a word no self-respecting historian ever uses. That price was the disappearance of the small farmer, the small farmer in lowland, arable farming England that is, as the pastoral hill farmer continued to hang on in the Peak District, in the Yorkshire Dales and on the Yorkshire Moors, in Cumbria, and in Wales.

All are agreed, that the small arable farmer, the classic peasant farmer of twelfth- and thirteenth-century England, was a specie of the fairly distant past by 1700. He was replaced by big yeomen farmers on the one hand, and landless labourers on the other. There were far more of the latter than the former, so the scene was set for commercial and industrial revolution. The fifteenth century was the crucial period that marked the profound restructuring of English rural society. Then it was, in a time of prosperity, that the old egalitarianism of a peasant culture disintegrated. It was not only that rural society became heavily differentiated, pulling apart at either end of the social scale. Men and women were also, and for the first time, highly mobile, seeking out the best land, looking for better, more highly paid jobs.

Movement to the depleted towns of England continued apace. Rents in towns were low when houses stood empty, as at Oxford, where the founders of New College and Magdalen College took the chance to buy up urban property for their new foundations. And, as ever, London was the magnet it had always been, the time when Richard Whittington arrived to find that the city streets were really paved with gold. Conversely, the turnover of village populations was often 100 per cent in less than 100 years, as families moved in and out again. Such mobility broke up established village communities and made it easy for yeomen and gentlemen 'on the make' to ride roughshod over community rights. It was not often that families were thrown off the land, but it happened more frequently than some historians would have us believe. This was precisely the time when Thomas More was condemning such antisocial behaviour in the first book of *Utopia* (1516).

The appearance of the fifteenth-century English countryside would not have told the full story. The dilapidated appearance of many villages, down to half their size; the reduction of hamlets to a single farmstead; the shrivelled look of hundreds of small and middling market towns, and the tumbledown nature of manor houses, did not reveal the whole truth. One or two farms along the village street, or sometimes out on their own enclosed fields, looked brand new, and were: think of the Wealden houses of Kent, for example, the homes of flourishing yeomen farmers. Or think of the spanking new and swanky churches of South West England, of the Cotswolds, of Norfolk, Suffolk and northern Essex. These were built out of the profits of woollen cloth, *not* wool, of malted barley, for beer, of cattle farming, of cod fishing off Iceland, and out of the spoils of the Hundred Years' War. Such grand churches are still called wool Churches. It would be more accurate to call them cloth, mutton or war churches. If it is true that in a capitalist culture we are condemned to live on what amounts to a building site, then fifteenth-century England should, at the very least, be thought of as proto-capitalist, even if more buildings were falling down than were being put up.

I have said that by 1430 or thereabouts freedom, in the sense of personal liberty, was no longer a matter of concern to the English peasantry, a peasantry that was transmuting into something else once personal liberty had been achieved. What was important, what it sometime seems took the place the cause of freedom had vacated, was a popular demand for good government. This is an interlude of a kind and it coincides with what are called the War of the Roses. Perhaps it was the new sense of sturdy independence that carried lesser gentry, yeomen and husbandmen, as well as a broad cross section of townsmen, into the political arena.

Indeed, they were foremost amongst those who joined the ranks of Jack Cade's rebels in 1450 and marched on London to voice their grievances. These were not social, nor were they economic, nor did the legal profession on this occasion come in for criticism. It was the government of Henry VI which, it was widely considered, had let the nation down, abroad as well as at home. The Hundred Years' War was nearing its end, and it may never have been winnable, but the government's critics, from the mighty Duke of York down to the mysterious Jack Cade, believed otherwise. Corruption, if not treason, in high places was to blame, and in a series of proclamations the corrupt were named, and their sins set out in detail. The king's chief minister, William de la Pole, Duke of Suffolk, and a number of other advisors to the Crown were set upon and murdered, and the Commons in Parliament joined in the criticism of a government that had run out of both money and ideas.

(In this connection we should note that unlike 1381, the rebels of 1450 wrote everything down; we should note it because literacy in English was becoming widespread, perhaps 40 per cent of the population could read, and in Bristol, Norwich, Coventry, York, and especially London, more than that. This is as powerful testimony to the precociousness of English culture, as capitalist farming is to the early flowering of the English economy.)

Cade's revolt was not the only popular protest against the failures of the Lancastrian and Yorkist governments. There were a series of other demonstrations in the 1450s, and Richard the so-called Kingmaker, Earl of Warwick, could count until the very end on the support of 'ordinary folk' in the south east of England when he took up arms against one or another king. Richard III's speedy departure from the political scene will be debated for as long as there is historical debate, but it seems that revulsion among people of all ranks of society at his responsibility for the murder of the young princes in the Tower meant that they did nothing to prevent his fall. Englishmen, on any and every reading of the politics of the fifteenth century, were, it seems, well enough informed to make up their own minds on political issues. It was not only the fullness of their purses they cared about. How war was conducted, how violence was contained in towns and the countryside, how the king distributed lands and office, all these were matters of concern as much as that old perennial: taxation. However, this period was a happy interlude between legal subjection and economic subservience. The onset of the latter as the sixteenth century got into its stride will be the topic which brings the second part of this chapter to a close.

Rural society had been dislocated by the Black Death. For a time, that dislocation worked to the advantage of many, probably most, of those who lived in the English countryside, who composed, we must remember, 90 per cent of the overall population. It was, however, only for a time. The so-called 'Golden Age of the English Peasantry' was short – it was also an Indian Summer. There would be no going back to it. Once landlords recovered themselves, once population first stabilized and, from around 1500, began to grow; once wages began to decline and prices to rise, the situation returned to what Marc Bloc regarded as the 'norm', to the small man being at the mercy of the big one.

The turn-around happened very quickly, and for two reasons. On the one hand there was much less bread – it was more bread and less porridge now – than there might otherwise have been because so much of England, notably the Midlands, the former bread basket of the country, and particularly of London and the Home Counties, had been put down to grass. Nor was that grass reconverted to arable while the cloth trade boomed, as it did until the slump of the 1560s. Commercial farming had come to stay, whatever the state of the economy. On the other hand, there were more people who did not grow their own bread. Subsistence farming had not entirely disappeared, but in 1500 all those who had given up such a gruelling way of life for good wages as an agricultural labourer in the previous century, and they comprised possibly a third of the rural population, began to feel the pinch as wages plummeted and prices of all commodities rose sharply.

This pulling in opposite directions soon meant that the indigent became a problem for the authorities, from the parish all the way up to parliament. Legislation to curb arable being converted to grass was enacted as early as 1487, and further legislation followed. As for the poor, they were far more mobile than the poor of 1300. Rooted in the village they had been fed, or not fed, by their fellow villagers when lean years struck, whereas this now rootless population so panicked the parliamentary classes that slavery and branding were at one point in the 1530s recommended as a solution.

Again, it should not be forgotten that there were by that time many workers in the cloth industry, cottage industry though that was, who were often laid off in the slack years and had long been habituated to wandering from Bradford to Bristol, from Coventry to Coggeshall, in search of work. Government in the turbulent 1530s was desperately afraid of the reputation of these traditionally independent spirits. It was thought that they were bound to cause trouble, and government, in an age which through its own policies had become one of religious controversy and dissent, was hypersensitive to the prospect of rebellion and revolt. It had reason to be.

In 1517, there had been a major disturbance in London, when foreigners had been attacked and killed. Popular xenophobia was a sign of the times. It had been an upper-class concern in earlier centuries, brought into being by wars against the Welsh and the Irish in the first instance, and by lost wars against the Scots and French thereafter. St George was a saint for aristocratic warriors. How his cult came to be imposed on the remainder of the population remains something of a mystery. No doubt, victory at Agincourt helped in the process. It was a victory which the English could have done without. There had also been resistance to Cardinal Wolsey's Amicable Grant of 1525. A new scheme of taxation, even if fairer in its application, always unnerves those who have to pay, or believe they may have to. Thus, one way or another, early Tudor governments were always looking for trouble, and looking for it they found it in a major way in 1536.

Conclusion

The Pilgrimage of Grace of 1536 was the closest any government came to be toppled by the people before the seventeenth century. The frequent usurpations of the later Middle Ages and the killing of four out of five fifteenth-century kings, an English habit not approved of abroad, does not demonstrate the weakness of English political institutions. On the contrary, it shows how well-founded these institutions were; they could easily take the strain. The Lady Jane Grey affair, and attempted usurpation, was a seven days' wonder, a storm in a teacup compared with the Pilgrimage of Grace.

What caused the people of the north, of the country beyond the Trent, the old stamping ground of Robin Hood, to rise up against a Westminster government they regarded as more than bad and bureaucratic? For the good Catholic folk of Lincolnshire, Yorkshire, Lancashire and Cumbria, it seemed that Thomas Cromwell, Thomas Cranmer, and their colleagues on Henry VIII's Privy Council, a.k.a. the Cabinet, were bent on destroying a way of life we might want to call religious but which was much more than that.

Religion is always more than religion pure and simple, neither of which things, even in a monastery or a mystic's cell, can it ever be, religion being nothing if it is not about the here and now, about everyday things. The Pilgrimage of Grace, historians believe, was primarily about religion, the everyday religion of ordinary parishioners, which those parishioners believed was under threat from southerners who were ideologically unsound, and bent on enriching themselves at the expense of the church. The uprising carried all before it, and was on such a scale that it had the widest political implications. The government faltered. It was only by lying and deceit, in which Henry himself took a leading part, that the credulous Pilgrims were dispersed. Once they were, the first excuse that came to hand was used to punish them severely; hundreds were hanged, including abbots and monks, towards whom Henry showed a vicious lack of mercy. The way in which the Pilgrimage of Grace was handled shows not only how rattled the government was, but also reveals the lengths to which a regime threatened by a popular uprising of a good half of its citizens will go to cling on to power. Did it change its policy? It did not.

We cannot leave it there. The 1530s were a turning point in English history. For one thing, capitalism had come to stay, capitalist farming that is. With the cloth industry the nation had embarked on its fateful course towards imperialism. Tudor exploration began as a search for better cod fishing grounds, continued with the hunting out of new markets for English cloth exports, and ended with the plantation of colonies that would take everything made in England. We were already on the way to becoming the nation of shopkeepers, industrialists and bank managers that was to be our fate until we were ruined, as such, by two world wars and the decay of a culture that is commercial and imperial. That said, the 1530s was also a turning point where religion was concerned, and more obviously, though it was R. H. Tawney who made the connection between religion and capitalism in a book that has stood the test of time better than most: *Religion and the Rose of Capitalism* published in that unfateful year 1926. It is not necessarily that capitalism requires Protestantism in order to make its way in the world. It is rather that the sort of Catholicism practised by the ordinary English man and woman in 1500 stood in the way of what Cromwell and Cranmer and their colleagues thought of as 'modernization'.

A perfect illustration of what they were up to is the abolition by parliamentary legislation in the 1530s of so many saint's days. Medieval and early modern peasants, those say painted by Bruegel, took every opportunity not to work; having to work for someone else may have played its part in this inclination. Play was the thing, not work. Every Saint's Day, like every Sunday, every baptism, wedding, or funeral was an occasion for taking the day off. Moreover, every Saint's Day had its Vigil, just as every Sunday had its Saturday, and every Christmas its twelve days. It has been calculated that in the Middle Ages there were almost as many holidays as there were working days. The Church concurred in all this, but a Church that countenanced, indeed encouraged 'idleness', a new word coined by the Reformers, was not to be tolerated when it was work above all that was required of the nation's citizens, citizens who were liable to be up to the devil's work when they became idle 'hands'.

Of course, the devil had always been ready to enter empty heads. That is why the monks and nuns were always busy, an active life and a contemplative mind being two sides of the same coin. That was not how Henry VIII and his councillors saw things. Monks and nuns at prayer were not monks and nuns at work. For prayer is the other touchstone of the magnitude of the changes taking place in England at the close of the Middle Ages. We shall end this chapter with its transference from the centre to the periphery of the Englishman's understanding of the world.

It is above all prayers for the dead that went missing at the Reformation. This was a profound change, for it meant that the dead, too, went missing, missing from this world. Unlike the poor the dead, it seems, are not always with us. The profundity of the change lies in the emphasis on the here and now that the elimination of the dead from the day-to-day life of the living entailed. The change heralded the beginning of the development, a capitalist development, that has culminated in a concentration on instant gratification. Prayer for the dead is a leap of faith. How do we know that it achieves its purpose until we ourselves are dead? It is the very antithesis of the late-capitalist preoccupation with immediate success and reward. Heaven, in another phrase, has to be now.

It is obvious what this has to do with freedom, or rather bondage. All those virtues that accompanied a faith in the future that was beyond today, like patience, humility, reticence, and, above all, concern for others, typified, most obviously, in prayers for the dead, are ones that allow spiritual escape from emotional dependence; on the next gratification, which, as it turns out, is only one in a series, for the very existence of capitalism depends on each one of us wanting the next thing in the sequence, sold to us under the deceitful guise of it being better. Here, therefore, is the most terrible of all unfreedoms, the one that is a treadmill of desire for that which is designed not to satisfy, but to ensure the continuance of dissatisfaction, a new product of necessity being 'better' than the old.

What happened as the Middle Ages were hijacked into Modernity by the English Reformation was not promising for the future. It may be that Modernity had to make its appearance so that lesser freedoms – political, social, and even economic – might be achieved, but in the process something, probably much, possibly everything, was lost.

Chapter 2

The English Civil War and the Putney Debates

William Lamont

Introduction: Why Puritans went to War

In 1999 the historian Conrad Russell urged his fellow historians to make 'a very sharp division between the reasons why people fought the Civil War on the one hand, and its causes on the other.' Although Russell never mentioned him, there was a contemporary Puritan minister who was very sensitive to the distinction, Richard Baxter, who fought for Parliament against the King in the Civil War. Baxter served as a chaplain in the New Model Army, but he made no subsequent reference to what is commonly seen as the supreme example of radicalism in the famous Putney Debates within the army in 1647. We shall see that he is not alone in this neglect, and in this chapter we shall try to understand why.

Baxter wrote his own explanation of the causes of the Civil War in his memoirs, which were posthumously published in 1696. It is almost impossible to overstate their influence on future readings of what these events meant. Indeed, one historian went so far as to write of the 'almost religious reliance' which were imputed to them. One can see why. Here was a man who had fought for Parliament, but could at the end of his life perceive the War as a tragedy rather than a melodrama. He could now see that there were good men on both sides, and that the villains were those on either side who exploited differences. If Baxter had known then what we know now, he would have seen the case for neutralism.

It was only in retrospect, however, that he traced the long term causes of the war back to Tudor times, giving weight to the political, social and economic factors, as well as the religious. There was even some pop sociology thrown in, which would selectively be drawn on by later historians. Of course, there had been an earlier attempt to look back in 1659, when Baxter wrote *Holy Commonwealth*. The tone then was different and quite unrepentant. In 1659 he would have done exactly what he did in 1642. When the monarchy was restored in 1660 these sentiments caused him grave trouble, and he formally repudiated it in 1670. Nonetheless, the work was to become part of the Oxford Convocation's notorious 'burning of the books' in 1683, alongside the works of Hobbes and Milton.

Baxter never claimed in *A Holy Commonwealth* to be providing the detailed analysis of the origins of the Civil War, which he would offer later. His fatal Chapter 13, 'Of the late Warres', he explained, was his response to the question that many people had put to him since 1642, namely: 'By what Reasons was I moved to engage myself in the Parliamentary Warre?' This was Conrad Russell's distinction, and the answer Baxter gave to that question was the answer he gave for the rest of his life – not only in printed sources but prudentially in manuscripts which fortunately have survived. He would graphically describe the Great Fear prompted by the Irish Catholic Rebellion of October, 1641:

> When in time of peace they suddenly Murdered two hundred thousand, and told men they had the King's Commission to rise as for him that was wronged by this Parliament the very fame of the horrid murder, and the words of the many fugitives that escaped into Beggary in England ... and the English Papists going into the King was the main cause that filled the Protestant Armies. I well remember it cast such a fear that England would be used like Ireland, that all over the Countreys, the people oft sate up, and durst not go to bed for fear that the Papists should rise and Murder them.

For Puritans like Baxter, Liberty was not the main concern, but Popery was. Although there was no single 'Papist' conspiracy at court, whatever the pamphleteers may have said, there were certainly

Catholic intrigues from at least the 1630s until the outbreak of the war which inspired the rumours that made a belief in a 'Popish Plot' plausible. Many of these intrigues were in fact self-contradictory. Most centred on Charles's Catholic wife, Henrietta Maria. Charles I still awaits the biographer who can explain to our satisfaction his relationship to his wife, and to these intrigues. One thing, however, is clear. It is that, in 1642, a high proportion of the governing class thought that they did, indeed, have a key to the mystery. The people at court who fuelled these suspicions were a motley crew: Henrietta Maria herself, Scottish Catholics, the minions of the Papal agent at her court, George Con, Jesuits, seculars, anti-Richelieu exiles, Spanish sympathizers and others – all with different agendas. These intrigues must be placed in the context of the Thirty Years' War. It is the recognition of this European dimension to the problem (evident enough in contemporary sources) which makes the threat to English Protestantism posed by the numerically insignificant Roman Catholics one of substance, not illusion.

This is the context in which the controversy about the Antrim Commission would acquire such significance. Who was the Earl of Antrim? He was the Irish Catholic, Randal MacDonnell, who had married Catherine, widow of the Duke of Buckingham, and herself a Catholic convert. Until moving to Ireland, late in 1638, with her new husband, the Duchess occasionally carried messages between Con and Archbishop Laud, who on one occasion had dreamed that he had helped England to be converted to Catholicism, and on another that he had gone to bed with Buckingham. He was equally contrite about both.

As early as the beginning of 1638, Antrim had presented a plan to Charles I and Henrietta Maria to take an army of his Ulster clansmen (he claimed to be able to raise 10,000) to Scotland to crush the Protestant rebellion there. When the King needed his help, in May 1639, Antrim was not able to honour his promise. But later? He was one of the leaders of the Irish Catholic rebellion, in October 1641, and a personal friend of its leader, Phelim O'Neill. Initially, the rebel leaders in Ireland, like O'Neill and Maguire, had claimed royal backing for the uprising. Later they withdrew these claims.

Even so, in 1643, opponents made the point that Charles I only publicly dissociated himself from the October rebels as late as January 1642, and that there were no initiatives from him in the interim months to reflect the horror he would belatedly express at the rebels' actions. It was as late as 8 April 1642, before he chastised 'those wicked and detestable rebels', and by that time it would be the minimum that could be expected of him. Most damaging of all was when Antrim, himself a prisoner in 1650, revealed in a series of depositions the extent of the understandings between himself and Charles I in 1641.

These original depositions have not survived. Nor has the correspondence between Charles and Antrim. Nonetheless, Antrim's biographer is convinced that his understanding with Charles was genuine. Other scholars are less sure. What is not in dispute is the fillip given after the Restoration to the conspiracy theory when Charles II pardoned Antrim because, it is said, he recognized the understanding that had existed between Antrim and his father.

Edmund Ludlow, a Cromwellian general, would expose the Antrim Commission in his influential Restoration pamphlet *Murder Will Out*. Now that the original manuscript of Ludlow's memoirs has, in part, been recovered, it is possible to document the good use to which he put the Antrim revelations. In the feverish Popish Plot atmosphere of 1679, the Antrim allegations were widely drawn upon. Indeed, when Edward Borlase wanted to cite them in his projected history of Irish Catholic crimes, the censor, Sir Roger L'Estrange, moved smartly to expunge them. The Antrim Commission was the fatal, circumstantial link between the Stuart monarchy and the Irish Catholic rebels.

The Irish rebellion of October 1641 was the *chronological* prelude to the Civil War in England. Puritans like Baxter also saw it as the *logical* prelude. The more we understand the mentality of English Protestants in 1641, the less easy it is to see Baxter as a special case. Was he a paranoid personality, sniffing papists under the bed? On the contrary, he got on well with individual Catholics, would quote Catholic authorities such as Aquinas with reverence, and at the end of his life dared to argue that the Pope was not Antichrist. The last was a brave declaration from a seventeenth-century Protestant. Here was no simple-minded Protestant bigot. Indeed, we do not have to postulate simple-minded bigotry when measuring the depth of seventeenth-century anti-Catholic feeling.

Anti-Catholicism drew on complex, political and eschatological roots in this period. A local study in Staffordshire showed, in the run-up to the Civil War, the excellent relations at a *personal level* that existed between Catholics and Protestants. This was not all. One historian has established that something like 90 per cent of English Catholics stayed neutral when the Civil War broke out. Indeed, John Pym, that master player of the anti-Roman card, made a very significant speech to the Commons on 17 July 1640, when he gave this warning to sentimental colleagues: 'Wee must not looke at a Papist as hee is in himselfe *but as hee is in the body of the Church.*' The distinction was critical. Pym was asking his colleagues not to be distracted by the amiable personal qualities of individual Catholics, but instead to concentrate on what it was that they stood for.

The fact that Pym should have to couch his appeal in these terms is remarkable, and points up the ambivalence of the whole concept. Research confirms what our reading of Pym's warning would suggest. Anti-Catholicism was not a constant tap, waiting to be switched on and off. The city of Plymouth was seriously damaged by a great fire in 1637 without unleashing a violent anti-Catholic pogrom. But peace could also be deceptive. Staffordshire's good relations could not survive suspicion of the Crown's policies. Hence the traumatic shock of the Irish Catholic rebellion, and the significance of the rebels' claims to have the blessing of the King.

Thus, on 5 November 1641, a very good day to choose, Pym could urge on his colleagues, with none of the qualifications of his July 1640 speech, the importance of sending the Scottish army to fight the rebels in Northern Ireland, and the need for 'ill councillors' to be removed from Parliament, before Parliament took further steps to relieve Ireland, itself the pretext for the Militia Ordinance which caused the decisive breach between King and Parliament.

The Civil War is not to be explained away simply as a Popish Plot writ large, but the religious dimension is the element most likely to be underrated. There is a very understandable reason for this. When we think of the English Civil War, our tendency is to compare it with events like the French or Russian Revolutions. (In a lecture tour of China in 1986, I tried to persuade my hosts that we had had a revolution too, but with little success.) Indeed, there seems to be something demeaning and reductionist in putting it in the context of Popish Plots. Now, in terms of its *consequences,* I would argue (against my Chinese hosts and others) that 1642–9 has a place alongside 1789 and 1917. But in terms of its *origins,* there is a lot to be said for placing the English Civil War in the sequence of anti-Catholic outbursts which racked seventeenth-century England.

There was a time when the Great Plague of 1665 was seen as a violent and unique aberration. Historians would now explain why it remained so long in the historical memory was because it was the last major outbreak of a disease which recurred throughout the century. So too with the Popish Plot of 1678–9. Here was no aberrant outbreak of hysteria. Titus Oates could, and did, draw upon earlier material linking Popish Plots and the Crown, right down to the smallest details, from the Guy Fawkes Plot, the Habernfield Plot and the Irish Rebellion. Shaftesbury, the Whig grandee, could play on the same fears that Pym had done earlier. We saw the Antrim story being purveyed by men like Borlase and Ludlow in 1678–9 precisely because it was at one with the psychology of 1641, of which Baxter gave graphic witness.

It is not wrong, therefore, to pursue parallels between the English Civil War and the French and Russian Revolutions in terms of the issues they raise. Yet, to draw parallels between the English Civil War, the Gunpowder Plot before, and the Popish Plot after, may actually take us close to the mentality of the men who took up arms to save their country from popery. Germane as the issue was, however, it seems that it was never directly raised at the Putney Debates of 1647, at least in the minutes of the meetings that have survived.

The Putney Debates

Tony Benn gives a marvellously indiscreet memory of a Cabinet debate in 1975:

> Jim (Callaghan) reported that in Portugal, the Communist Party had infiltrated the army and 200 officers met every Friday at 10am and went on until late at night – I whispered to Michael (Foot) that it sounded like the Putney debates of 1647. Jim suggested that junior ministers be sent to Portugal to sustain the new regime. Very interesting; obviously Portugal is now undergoing the same experience as we had during the English Civil War, and most of today's Cabinet would have been on the side of the King.

In broad terms, Benn's analogy is a good one. At the end of the first Civil War, in 1646, the King had been defeated, but his conquerors did not know what to do with him. Jim's Cabinet might have had a majority who were on the King's side but, and it is here that the analogy does not hold, at Putney *nobody* was on the King's side, and at the same time *everybody* was. Charles I was universally mistrusted, but also indispensable. Or was he, as a few were beginning to dare to propose? Moreover, Putney was not part of a series of regular caucus meetings organized by radical infiltrators on the Portuguese model. It was the generals of the victorious New Model Army, which had then been in existence for two years, who had set up the new General Council of the Army, with two officers and two soldiers chosen from each regiment. From 9 September 1647 onwards they held meetings on Thursdays in Putney Parish Church.

As early as April, soldiers had begun electing what they called 'agitators' to secure the redress of their grievances. On 18 October they produced their first manifesto, *The case of the armie truly stated*, under the signatures of agents from five regiments, and presented it to the Lord General of the Army, Sir Thomas Fairfax. Fairfax regarded this challenge as so serious that he believed that it must be put before the General Council presided over by Oliver Cromwell and his son-in-law, Henry Ireton. On 27 October the General Council was presented with a new and more radical case for change,

An Agreement of the People, which became the document debated at Putney. The generals, realizing how much was at stake, directed the General Council's secretary, William Clarke, to record the debates.

Like *The case of the army truly stated, An Agreement of the People* was published over the names of the agents of the five regiments. There is no gazumping by a different set of soldiers. There is common ground, clearly part of a common strategy, and yet both content and style are different. Some of the key points in the first paper – the dissolution of Parliament, to be followed by biennial parliaments elected by all 'freeborn' adult males – are replicated in the second. What was different in the second was the proposal of a new constitution to be legitimized by the personal assent of each and every one of the sovereign people, at least initially to be implemented by force.

Cromwell's rejection of the document was on grounds of its anarchy, one Swiss canton opposing another, and of the dubiety of the agitators' claim to speak for the sovereign people. Even so, Cromwell and Ireton did not seek to reject it *in toto*, and acknowledged some good things in it. It is a mistake to see officers and critics at Putney staring at each other across an abyss, despite profound differences. What emerges from the soldiers' pamphlets and petitions is a concern about arrears of pay, certainly, but also recognition of their 'honour' impugned by Parliament's disbanding of their regiments and conscripting them to serve in Ireland. Their constant refrain was that they were no mercenary army.

In *An Agreement*, the fourth clause, the concept of the sovereignty of the people, listed powers reserved to the people themselves, the second being the abolition of conscription, the first that 'matters of religion' should be left to the individual conscience. Cromwell could have said Amen to both, and the fact that he could say it was another bond with his critics. In prayer together they sought to determine the hand of God, the most unsettling thing about Putney to the twenty-first-century mind, yet the most commonplace to the seventeenth-century Puritan one. (A notable exception was the Leveller, William Walwyn, and his cynicism about prayer was one of his many traits condemned by his peers.)

There were three recorded days of debate: 28 and 29 October, and 1 November. What is less well known is that there were four meetings with no minutes (2, 5, 6, and 8 November). Did Cromwell and Ireton order Clarke not to keep a record on these days? And if so, why not? We don't know. One possibility is that during these closed sessions they debated the end of monarchy. Even as late as 1647 the idea was almost inconceivable. The Putney Debates would be wound up without any formalized decisions, the King would take flight and lead the Scots into the Second Civil War, there would be another defeat and another capture. Kings have been removed in our past history, but by palace coup, deposition or assassination. 1649 was totally different: the public trial of Charles Stuart, 'that man of blood'.

Here is an irony of history. The prime movers of regicide were the Army officers, led by Ireton, and typically, later and more equivocally, by Cromwell. Their opponents would be Levellers like Lilburne, who was not at Putney, and Sexby, who was. In 1647, the Levellers' public demands had gone no further than ending the royal veto on legislation. The recorded debates throw up the more familiar picture of Ireton defending property, and the solemnity of agreements, against Wildman and Rainborough, and again typically, Cromwell supporting him later and equivocally. It is in this context that one speculates about the minutes that were not taken.

Perhaps we shouldn't. What we have, as Benn pointed out, is the record of a thinking army, like Castro's in Cuba, Nasser's in Egypt, or indeed like Portugal's in 1975. In the free-thinking exchanges which Clarke did record, we glimpse democracy on the march and rejoice at Rainborough's great plea:

> I thinke that the poorest hee that is in England hath a life to lead as the greatest he, and therefor truly, Sir, I thinke itt's cleare, that every man that is to live under a Government ought first by his owne consent, to putt himself under that Government; and I do think that the poorest man in England is not at all bound in a strict sense to that government that hee hath not had a voice to put himself under.

We would gratefully settle for that, were it not for three doubts that cling to our Clarke legacy. I will deal with each of them in turn. The first is, how far we can trust Clarke? The second is why did Tom Paine, our greatest homegrown revolutionary, never mention Rainborough or the Putney Debates? The third is why does Putney warrant, in some perceptions, only two cheers for democracy but three for liberty?

How far can we trust Clarke?

Perhaps we come to the debates with the wrong expectations. We envisage a formal gathering with the secretary taking his leisured notes. A good corrective is to be found in the best film ever made portraying the seventeenth century: Kevin Brownlow's 1975 film on Winstanley the Digger. There we see Rainborough at Putney shouting out his immortal, fugitive words against a competitive hubbub of noise. We don't even see, but can imagine, the poor clerk trying to get it all down. Perhaps it wasn't just one man. We know, for instance, that three shorthand writers, one of whom was Clarke, were present at Charles I's execution to record his last words. It is probable, but there is no proof, that Clarke headed a team of three or four who would pool their understandings at the end of each session. In 1650, Clarke accompanied Cromwell on his Scottish campaign, and stayed with Monck, general of the Commonwealth army in Scotland, until 1660.

It was only in 1973 that it was established that Clarke used the Thomas Shelton shorthand favoured also by Pepys. In 1662, Clarke began the task of copying out his shorthand notes of 15 years earlier, and having some difficulties with them! When he was killed in the Second Dutch War in 1666 he had only completed the process up to March, 1651. A specialist researcher, Frances Henderson, has cracked the Putney code, and is completing the formidable task of deciphering Clarke's records of Cromwell's Scottish campaign. His son, George, inherited Clarke's papers. He was a don at All Souls, Oxford, until his death in 1736, and willed his father's papers not to his own college but to Worcester College, as a result of some internecine academic feud. We now know much more than we did about the text, but still don't know what Clarke was working from as he compiled his Worcester College manuscript. Frances Henderson, who should know if anyone does, warns against treating it as anything like a 'tape recording' of the debates themselves.

Why did Tom Paine forget the Putney Debates?

One might have expected Tom Paine to have been steeped in the Putney Debates. They don't even get a mention from him. Instead he explains the source of his commitment to democracy in these terms:

> So far from taking any ideas from Locke or anybody else, it was the expression of a man John Bull in England, about the year 1773, that first caused me to turn my mind to systems of government in England. In speaking of the then King of Prussia, called the Great Frederick, he said; 'This is the right sort of man for a King for he has a deal of the Devil in him.' This set me to think if a system of government could not exist that did not require the devil, and I succeeded without any help from any body.

Perhaps we like our heroes to be modest, shy, gee-shucks characters, to be played on the screen by James Stewart? That very much was not Tom Paine. A contemporary said of him, 'He knew all his own writings by heart, and nothing else.' He knew a great deal else. He had certainly read Milton, and almost certainly Harrington and Rousseau. If he pretended otherwise it was not a psychological flaw in his character so much as a forensic necessity. His genius as a journalist, and genius he certainly was, was inseparable from his jettisoning of past traditions and authorities, and speaking to the ordinary reader as if he were a neighbour on the other side of the fence exchanging self-evident truths.

The Norman Yoke was a powerful radical myth, and Clarke picks up numerous references to it at Putney. This was the idea that arbitrary rule was an alien import from a Norman bastard King: it still had resonance with the Chartists of the mid-nineteenth century, and the newly formed Labour Party in 1900. Magna Carta was the guarantor of pre-Norman liberties, and socialism was Saxon. But there were Levellers, like Walwyn, the probable part-author of *An Agreement of the People,* who thought that fellow leader Lilburne was too fond of precedents and traditions. There were even Levellers who referred to Magna Carta. Walwyn and Paine would have sympathized.

But Paine's neglect of Putney turns out not to have been killed, but based on ignorance – an ignorance which is universally shared. This is what many commentators on Putney missed: from 1647 to 1736, the Clarke papers were in the possession of William and then George; from 1736 to 1891 they were tucked away forgotten, in a Worcester College cupboard. Even in contemporary newspapers there had been little speculation about Putney. It slipped out of the historical memory. A vivid illustration was provided by a recent commemoration of the debates in Putney Church itself. The very good historian who chaired the day's session set his panel six questions which he wanted answered by the end of the day. One was to examine the eighteenth and nineteenth centuries, reception of Putney. To this there could be only one answer: there wasn't any, at least until 1891, unless, that is, larceny had been perpetrated on a grand scale in that interim period on the cupboard of a small Oxford college.

What happened in 1891? The librarian of Worcester College, Henry Pottinger, mentioned rather diffidently to a young visiting historian, Charles Firth, that there were some papers in a cupboard that he might care to look at. One can imagine Firth's excitement when he realized the treasure he had unearthed. He put his find to good use, publishing the Clarke papers for the Camden Society. He did not try to crack the Clarke code, but in all other respects he did a scholarly job. The documents were not introduced separately but were referred to in a long Preface. There was no index or list of contents. The Putney Debates were not mentioned as such in the Preface. The first, austere heading was: 'Att the generall Council of Officers att Putney 28 October, 1647.' One can hardly imagine a less reader-friendly introduction.

Firth was generous in communicating his discoveries to fellow scholars, and they gradually percolated through to larger text books.

There was a missed opportunity however in 1891 to engage with a wider public, and outside the academy general readers were left in the dark. We welcomed the launch of an ambitious collaborative enterprise in 2007: the publication of a million words of a little-known seventeenth-century Puritan called Roger Morrice. His shorthand code has again been cracked by Frances Henderson. He will inevitably be claimed as another Pepys, which he isn't, for there isn't one, but artfully the publishers have, more modestly, seized upon a chance remark by Morrice that he wouldn't dream of going to Tunbridge Wells because of its sleazy reputation. They circulated this story in advance to a range of newspapers, and were rewarded with good coverage, and in one case a light, witty third leader on the vagaries of stereotypes, in a so-called paper of record. This is the publicity launch that the Putney Debates, lost in the academic embrace, never had.

Two Cheers for Democracy, Three for Liberty?

One man in 1928 recognized the anomaly and worked incessantly to rectify it. His name was A. D. Lindsay, Master of Balliol College, Oxford. In that year, he went as far as to claim that 'our modern discussions of democracy' begin with Putney. Yet the ordinary reader was starved of easy access to the debates themselves. From 1736 to 1891, they lay neglected in a cupboard of Worcester College, Oxford. To be rescued by publication in the proceedings of the Camden Society was hardly exposure to the merciless gaze of the media. Yet Lindsay felt that that was what was needed. He had the foresight to see that England was entering a decade when democracy was to receive its supreme challenge. And ten years later, everything clicked into place.

The Royal Historical Society, which owned the copyright of Clarke's minutes, agreed to a publication along the lines of Lindsay's recommendation. Firth, now Sir Charles, Grand Old Man of Putney studies, and practically everything else in the seventeenth century, gave the project his blessing, and J. M. Dent agreed to publish it. All that was needed was an editor, and one was found in A. S. P.

Woodhouse. In his foreword to the first 1938 edition of the revised Clarke papers, *Puritanism and Liberty*, Lindsay conveyed his over-whelming sense of gratitude: 'we were fortunate to get Professor Woodhouse.' And so we were.

Woodhouse, no more than Firth before him, attempted to crack Clarke's shorthand, but in all other respects he produced a scholarly, accessible volume, this time with a list of contents, an index, and a long and thoughtful Introduction that has worn well. This volume has gone through many editions, and never been out of print. Lindsay went so far as to say that Woodhouse had produced 'something much more complete than I had originally dared to hope'. It is a fair bet that Benn, in his whispered exchange in Cabinet with Foot, would have been drawing upon readings from Wood-house, rather than Firth, just like the rest of us.

Lindsay and Woodhouse were alike in seeing Putney above all as the school for democracy. Each recognized the part the other played in advancing that insight. In his Introduction, Woodhouse praised Lindsay's own early work, *The essentials of democracy,* for his claim there that the seventeenth-century congregation was the model for twentieth-century democracy. Lindsay for his part commended Woodhouse to those who wished 'to be able to give a reason for their democratic faith'. He put that faith to a personal test when he fought the famous 1938 Oxford by-election as an Independent candidate against Appeasement, and won a notable moral victory, but not the seat, against his Tory opponent, Quintin Hogg. In his *Picture Post* report of 5 November 1938, Tom Har-risson quoted one middle-aged woman voter: 'Lindsay's not right opposing Chamberlain. You could have understood Labour doing it, but he's supposed to be an educated man.' How tempted Lindsay must have been to press into her hands Shaw's *Intelligent Woman's Guide to Democracy,* or now Woodhouse's *Puritanism and Liberty.*

Would then it have been better if Woodhouse had entitled his work *Puritanism and Democracy*? We can see, actually, why he chose the title he did. Woodhouse was in the long tradition of transatlantic scholarship which traced its liberty roots back to its Puritan origins (other examples of this from many, William Haller's *Tracts on Liberty in the Puritan Revolution,* of 1934, and W. K. Jordan's four-volume work *The development of religious toleration in England,* from 1932 to 1940).

This matters because Woodhouse gave more than a title; he gave a theme into which Putney is subsumed. The debates amount to about a third of the entire volume (Part I, pp. 1–124), while the Whitehall debates of December 1648, and January 1649 (Part II, pp. 125–78) are, unlike Putney, focused explicitly on religious liberty. The editor then selected extracts from contemporary pamphlets to fit around his chosen theme (Part III, pp. 179–473): 'Puritan Views on Liberty'. This section is by far the longest in the volume. Title and packaging combine to make liberty seem to be the most important legacy of Putney.

Woodhouse, however, was too good a scholar to be entirely happy with this elision. Instead he acknowledges its fragility in his Introduction:

> a concern for liberty does not appear to be a constant feature of the Puritan mind, and that it runs counter to another of the most universally recognized of traits, the passionate zeal for positive reform, with the will, if necessary, to dragoon men into righteousness – or the semblance of righteousness.

A concern for liberty could not be said to be Lindsay's highest priority in 1938. In his Foreword he commended Woodhouse not to all of his contemporaries, but to those of them who wished 'to be able to give a reason for their democratic faith'. More than this, he hoped it would be read so as 'to stop the mouths and pens of others'. But who were they, these others? They were those 'who produce facile refutations of the fundamental ideas of democracy'. Stopping mouths and pens does not sound like a hymn to liberty. Nor should that surprise us in 1938. What was important in pamphlet or at by-election hustings was to get the democratic message across.

When a new edition of Woodhouse was produced in 1950, Lindsay provided a postscript to his original Foreword. Woodhouse had said in his Introduction: 'there is in Puritanism a possibility of autocracy as well as a possibility of democracy'. Lindsay now seized on these words and invested them with a new meaning. The enemy then had been fascism. Now it was an autocracy *which called itself a democracy* (my italics). With the 'rise and spread of an entirely new idea of democracy in eastern Europe', Lindsay argued that Woodhouse's study had now assumed 'a new importance'. In that light, Putney could be reassessed in 1950. The debates, Lindsay claimed, now show 'the fundamental connection between *western* democracy and liberty, and the opposition between democracy and any kind of totalitarianism' (my italics).

Perhaps it was on a caprice that Woodhouse had opted for *Puritanism and Liberty* rather than *Puritanism and Democracy*, but in the event how fortuitous! It was Cold War logic that the east's commitment to democracy should be seen as spurious, and the west's commitment to liberty as uncontroversial. Woodhouse, as we have seen, had his reservations about his Putney Puritans' commitment to either in 1938. And in that same year, R. H. Tawney published *Equality*, which gave the socialist case against an unreserved endorsement of liberty in the epigram: 'Freedom for the pike is death for the minnow.'

In the United States, by the end of the twentieth century, the strains in the Puritan connection with liberty were becoming all too apparent. The Rutherford Institute, with its 50 full-time staff and around 500 volunteer lawyers, had been set up in 1982 to defend religious liberties from the perceived threat from the secular state. In 1998, it saw its function to cleanse the White House of moral corruption. Thus within a matter of 16 years the Puritans' negative concept of liberty (freedom from) had been transformed into a positive concept of liberty (freedom to). Its members claimed to be in a direct descent from Samuel Rutherford, the seventeenth-century Scottish Presbyterian, whose name is honoured in the Institute's title. His writings feature in Woodhouse's long section on 'Puritan Views of Liberty', and the Institute's apologists try to tie him up with liberalism and Locke, although there is no evidence that Locke ever quoted, or even read, Rutherford.

Was it coincidence or Providence that in Washington on 3 and 4 October 1997, when scholars convened to commemorate the 350th anniversary of the Putney Debates in the Folger Library, the capital was taken over by an estimated half a million men and their sons in baseball caps? They called themselves the Promise Keepers, and were anti-gay, anti-abortion religious fundamentalists. On the subway, with a wife, but no son, and no baseball cap, I found myself not wholly persuaded of the unbreakable links between Puritanism and Liberty. Were these men and boys the heirs of Rutherford or, more pertinent to Putney, of Cromwell and Ireton?

Promise-keeping was no peripheral matter at Putney. Property, marriage, a new constitution – these were all tied up by Ireton to the core question which takes up such an inordinate amount of time on the first of what is, after all, only three recorded days of debate: should promises be kept? Students who initially thrill to the *concept* of the debates – the romance of the discovery of the papers, the great set-pieces on the franchise – are often turned off by the *reality*. Those wearisome arguments about what makes a covenant binding, those marathon prayer meetings to resolve issues, the readiness for God's sake, literally, to listen to each others' dreams – they all prompt a response on the lines of 'great about the franchise, pity about the Puritanism'.

I was asked once by the BBC to adapt the Putney Debates as a TV play. I wasn't the first, and won't be the last. It may one day even be done, but I, for one, couldn't see how to do it. Like students, potential audiences would come with expectations which the material can't satisfy. It is often a difficult read. It comes in fragmentary, disconnected form, for all the heroic retrieval efforts by Clarke and his colleagues, and much later by our cipher Queen, Frances Henderson, who nevertheless warns us that the finished product can never approximate in the slightest to a tape recording of the debates themselves. And it is set in terms of reference to the seventeenth-century Puritan mind which we can easily caricature. That in no way diminishes the importance of its discovery, even if from 1736 to 1891 they could have no direct influence on history. That is why I salute the brave film on the Digger, Winstanley, which includes the Putney Debates in its impressionistic display of muddle as, nevertheless, an integral explanation of what the English Revolution was about.

Woodhouse saved Putney from the cold, dead hand of the scholar. He then set it off on the wrong path when he subsumed it into his theme *of Puritanism and Liberty*. Lindsay compounded the error when he hailed the Putney Debates for their contribution to the Cold War. He was actually closer to the Puritan *mentalité* of 1647, not in 1950, but in 1938 when he let rip his own profound yearning 'to stop the mouths and pens' of those who badmouthed democracy. They are almost the verbatim sentiments of the Puritan root and branch minister, Thomas Wilson, in 1641: 'a pious man's greatest care is that vile persons that spake villainy may have their mouths stopped that the purity of discipline, very necessary to the constitution of the Church, may be introduced.'

When Lindsay, in 1950, gives us the Puritans as premature anti-Stalinists, elevating liberty above democracy, we know that, although Putney can offer us many different scripts, this one is plain wrong. That wrongness began as early as 1904–5 when the great sociologist, Max Weber, published his *The Protestant Ethic and the Spirit of Capitalism*. According to the American historian C. H. George, in 1968, this is what followed:

> much of the literature on puritanism has since Weber concentrated on determining the relationship of the undefined abstract 'puritanism' to such undefined or non-historical abstracts as 'capitalism', 'the spirit of capitalism', 'democracy', 'individualism', 'liberty', 'revolution', 'science', 'Anglicanism', 'progress', even 'modernity'.

Woodhouse is found guilty by George of what he calls 'manic abstractionism' in his 1952 article, 'Religion and some foundations of English democracy'. But a greater distortion still is perpetrated by the 'alchemist tricks' of scholars like Woodhouse (again), Haller and Jordan when they transmute 'the base stuff of puritan piety into the gold of egalitarianism, individualism and tolerance'.

It is against such alchemy – those Washington Promise Keepers of 1997! – that this chapter has been written.

Chapter 3

Colonial Wars and Liberal Imperialism: a History of Parliamentary Failure

John Newsinger

All colonial wars are based on lies. This is inevitable. Colonial wars are inevitably one-sided affairs involving an advanced country with a modern economy and military attacking a backward country that is, in comparison, virtually defenceless. The only way such ruthless aggression can be justified to domestic opinion is by lies. The lies differ, of course, according to the nature of the regime launching the war. In liberal democracies, the victim of colonial aggression is generally portrayed as a threat, sometimes as the actual aggressor, and the war is inevitably in the best interests of the 'native' population. Sometimes the war is to free them from tyranny, to bring them into the modern world and bestow the benefits of civilization, to introduce them to good governance or to the advantages of free trade, yesterday's version of globalization. They are killed, so to speak, for their own good.

What one has to do when studying colonial wars, both past and present, is to distinguish between the real, actual causes that prompt colonial aggression and the pretexts that are used to justify it. There is a world of difference between the justifications that governments present to their own people and the motives that actually drive them on. The two are never the same. What is both interesting and disturbing is how little the pretexts and justifications for colonial wars have changed over the last 150 years. In order to justify what are often more like technological massacres than wars, politicians lie, sometimes even to themselves, because they know that their own people would never support these adventures if they were told the truth.

Let us look at two particular episodes that took place in the nineteenth century. In the first, we see an unsuccessful attempt by the House of Commons to actually rein in a government committed to the most blatant colonial aggression, and in the second, the complete and abject collapse of a parliamentary majority elected specifically to oppose colonial aggression in the face of the government's decision to undertake such an adventure. While both these episodes occurred before the democratization of the franchise, nevertheless Britain was a constitutional monarchy and can be usefully described as having a liberal regime. What hardly any of the histories of the period face up to is the extent to which this liberal regime fronted for a predatory imperialism that carried massacre and slaughter throughout much of the world. What is particularly interesting with regard to our two chosen episodes is how many similarities there are between these acts of Liberal Imperialism and the New Labour Government's decision to participate in the United States' colonial aggression against Iraq in 2003. Let us first look at the Second Opium War (1857–8).

'Our Criminal Policy In The East'

The cause of the Second Opium War was British determination to open up China as a market. An earlier conflict, the First Opium War (1839–42), fought on behalf of powerful British narco-capitalists, had gone some way towards accomplishing this, but the Chinese still stubbornly refused to acknowledge their place in Britain's informal free-trade empire. The sticking point was the city of Canton. Although the Chinese had agreed to open it up to the British, popular hostility in which the Chinese authorities acquiesced, kept it closed. This was completely unacceptable. Another military demonstration was necessary to bring home to the Chinese how dangerous it was to defy the British, but a suitable pretext had to be found. This was finally provided by the Chinese arrest of the lorcha the *Arrow*, together with her crew, at Canton on 8 October 1856. The British consul at Canton, Harry Parkes, according to his biographer, very much an 'apostle of the Palmerstonian doctrine', protested against this action most vigorously on the grounds that the *Arrow* was registered at Hong Kong and therefore under British protection, and had, moreover, been flying the British flag when boarded. The Chinese, Parkes claimed, had actually laid hands on the flag and had lowered it! He demanded the release of the crew and an apology. The Chinese, concerned to avoid a confrontation, released the crew, but refused to apologize, insisting that the vessel had not been flying the flag. The pretext had been found.

Even though it was found that the *Arrow*'s Hong Kong registration had lapsed and that there were good grounds for suspecting her of involvement in piracy, the governor of Hong Kong, Sir John Bowring, decided on a military response. While he acknowledged to Parkes that it appeared 'on examination that the Arrow had no right to hoist the British flag', nevertheless larger issues were at stake. He wrote to Parkes: 'Can we not use this opportunity to carry the City Question? If so I will come up with the whole fleet. I think we have now a stepping-stone from which with good management we may move on to important consequences'. Parkes, who had almost certainly invented the claim that the flag had been lowered, similarly recognized that there were great issues at stake. He wrote to his missionary brother-in-law, that he saw 'the finger of One who rules the destinies of races clearly traceable in the whole affair'. It was no less than 'the cause of the West against the East, of Paganism against Christendom, and what may we not look to as the result? The opening of China indeed, I trust'. Lest any doubt remain that the *Arrow* incident was merely a pretext, one of Bowring's sons, Lewin, in an introduction to his father's *Autobiographical Recollections*, admitted that the incident was, in fact, seized on 'as a means to an end, that end being the free admission of foreigners to the city of Canton'. He regretted, as well he might, that 'a better cause for a quarrel was not found than the "Arrow" affair'.

Research by the historian John Wong has established that the whole affair of the lowered flag was almost certainly fiction, made up to justify a military response. And, indeed, this was widely rumoured at the time. Richard Cobden, the radical MP, told Henry Richard of the Peace Society that he had had information passed to him to the effect that 'we have been dealing with something very like falsehood in our official correspondence'. He was assured, he went on, that it was common knowledge 'on all sides' in Hong Kong 'that the Arrow lorcha had no flag flying at all'. Sexed-up pretexts for war are clearly nothing new. As for Bowring, taking advantage of the Chinese refusal to apologize, he sent the Royal Navy to destroy Chinese forts and to carry out a punitive bombardment of Canton. A memorial from the people of Canton to the British complained with considerable justice that:

> The late affair of the lorcha was a trifle; it was no case for deep-seated animosity as a great offence that could not be forgotten; yet you have suddenly taken up arms and for several days you have been firing shell, until you have burned dwellings and destroyed people in untold numbers .... What offence has been committed by the people of Canton that such a calamity should befall them?

Certainly, the men on the spot felt that they had plenty of justification for their actions, they had the support of Lord Palmerston's government, and, of course, the British community in China, missionaries included, was always prepared to endorse the shedding of Chinese blood. Back home, however, there was widespread outrage at war being waged on such a flimsy and dishonourable pretext. The government found itself in serious trouble.

It is worth here briefly considering the reputation and career of Sir John Bowring. He was not a reactionary, bloodthirsty Tory Imperialist, but a notable liberal intellectual with an international reputation. Bowring had been a close friend and disciple of Jeremy Bentham, who had died in his arms, and as his literary executor he had edited his eleven-volume *Collected Works*. He had edited the *Westminster Review*. As a radical MP, he had supported the People's Charter, championed decimalization, condemned the opium trade, called for the abolition of flogging in the Army, supported the revolutionary cause in Italy and Poland, defending the rights of refugees who had fled to Britain, and he had been actively involved in the Peace Society, the anti-war movement of the time. Bowring was a strong non-conformist, the author of the hymn, 'In the Cross of Christ I Glory'. Like many middle-class non-conformists, he conflated Christianity with Free Trade. Indeed, on one occasion, he had famously proclaimed that 'Jesus Christ is Free Trade and Free Trade is Jesus Christ'. Although regarded as a financial expert, it was Bowring's personal financial problems (he was ruined in the recession of 1847) that led to his ending up in China, first as consul in Canton and later as governor of Hong Kong. He began his governorship with great reformist intentions, but very quickly, his Hong Kong administration had become mired in scandal and corruption. As for the Chinese population of the colony, Bowring imposed what amounted to a state of martial law on them.

According to that keen observer Justin McCarthy, as far as his friends were concerned there was nothing in Bowring's

> previous habits of life, nothing in the associations and friendships by which he had long been surrounded, nothing in his studies or his writings that warranted anyone in expecting that when placed in a responsible position in China at a moment of crisis he would have taken on him to act the part which aroused such a controversy. It would seem as if his eager self-conceit would not allow him to resist the temptation to display himself in the field of political action as a great English plenipotentiary, a master-spirit of the order of Clive or Warren Hastings, bidding England be of good cheer and compelling inferior races to grovel in the dust before her.

His former radical associates and friends concluded that he had sold himself to the opium merchants, something borne out by the fact that one of his sons became a partner in the most important of the opium trading companies, Jardine Matheson, and that they became Bowring's personal bankers. The reality was that it was impossible to govern Hong Kong without the support of the narco-capitalists. As for Bowring himself, he was, he insisted, an 'ardent lover of peace', he had 'been Secretary of the Peace Society, and had always taken an active part in promoting the peace movement', but the fact was that 'with barbarous – ay, and sometimes with civilized nations, the words of peace are uttered in vain'. These protestations, it is fair to say, convinced nobody and Bowring was to be condemned as the man responsible for manufacturing a war. Such is the fate of the Liberal Imperialist. Instead of being remembered as a reforming governor of Hong Kong, he is remembered as the architect of a colonial war initiated on so contemptible a pretext that it brought the government down.

Palmerston's government was wholeheartedly committed to military action to open up Canton as a preliminary to the renegotiation of Anglo-Chinese Treaty relations. What they found, however, was that they had become embroiled in conflict on a pretext that was widely derided and condemned as a disgrace. Bowring was the subject of general censure, but the government felt compelled to support the actions of the man on the spot, even though its members might have wished he had provided them with a more convincing pretext for war. The government faced votes of censure in both the Lords and the Commons. Palmerston sought the advice of the Attorney-General, Sir Richard Bethell, as to the legality of its conduct in China. George Douglas, the Earl of Argyll, provided a remarkable account of how Bethell lectured the Cabinet:

> There were occasional passages in his statement which seemed to me to indicate a very strong feeling against the overzealous civilian in China who had got us into a most serious difficulty. Before closing what he had to say, I recollect that he shook his head ominously, and indicated his opinion that a very serious case against us on the points of international law could be, and probably would be made out in the House of Commons ... We all thought it very evident that, were it not for his office, it would give him immense pleasure to take the part of leading counsel against us.

Attorneys-General were obviously of a different calibre in those days, or perhaps Palmerston had merely failed to appoint a close friend out of his depth to the post. In any event, the Cabinet decided to ignore Bethell's advice, deciding instead, that international law did not apply to what were characterized as 'barbarous nations'. A cynic might more accurately regard this as a decision that international law did not apply to countries that were incapable of defending themselves. It is worth noting that there were dissentient voices at all this, even within the Cabinet. The Chancellor of the Exchequer, Sir George Cornewall Lewis, made clear that if the Russians or the Americans had behaved as Britain had, 'we should be loud in our condemnation of so wanton an aggression'. As for the argument regarding 'barbarous nations', as Lewis pointed out, this doctrine 'may be made a cover for any aggression' with nations being labelled barbarous whenever it suited. Nevertheless, as a loyal party man, his objections remained within the government and he faithfully voted against the censure motion even though as he conceded, 'all the argument is on the other side'.

Bowring's conduct was debated in the Lords on 24 February 1857 with Lord Cranworth, the Lord Chancellor, actually driven to argue that it was impermissible for the Chinese to stop any vessel flying British colours, in their waters remember, whether it did so legally or not. As was pointed out at the time, this meant that any and every pirate had only to fly the British flag in order to be able to proceed unmolested. Nevertheless, the Lords stood by the government, voting against the censure motion by 146 votes to 110. In the Commons, two days later, the debate had a different result. Here, the censure, proposed by Richard Cobden, was carried by 263 votes to 247, despite all of Palmerston's patriotic bluster. He accused Cobden of believing that 'everything that was English was wrong, and everything that was hostile to England was right'. What his critics were proposing, he claimed, was 'to abandon a large community of British subjects at the extreme end of the globe to a set of barbarians – a set of kidnapping, murdering, poisoning barbarians'.

Patriotic bluster was not enough on this occasion, however. As Justin McCarthy observed:

> a growing conviction of the insufficiency of the defence set up for the proceedings on Canton influenced the great majority of those who spoke

and voted for Mr Cobden's motion. The truth is there has seldom been so flagrant and so inexcusable an example of high-handed lawlessness in the dealings of a strong with a weak nation. When the debate first began it was quite possible that many public men still believed some explanation or defence was coming forward ... As the discussion went on it became clear that there was no such defence or explanation. Men found their consciences coerced into a condemnation of Sir John Bowring's conduct. It was almost ludicrous when the miserable quibblings and evasions of British officials came to be contrasted with the cruelly clear arguments of the Chinese.

What Cobden described as 'our criminal policy in the East' had been repudiated by the Commons, and Palmerston responded by calling a general election. This quite momentous event, the overthrow of a British government for an act of colonial aggression, is, quite remarkably, completely marginalized in all the standard histories of this period. A rare attempt by a House of Commons majority to call a halt to an unprovoked colonial war that was to cost thousands of lives is passed over with hardly any discussion of its larger significance.

The opposition's triumph was short-lived. Palmerston fought an unashamedly jingoistic election campaign. He appealed, as the Colonial Secretary Sidney Herbert put it, to the 'public's national prejudices'. His widely circulated election manifesto made the issues absolutely clear: 'An insolent barbarian, wielding authority in Canton, has violated the British flag ...' In the May 1857 General Election, Palmerston won a great victory, with his supporters winning 367 seats, giving him an unreliable majority of 85. Many of his most prominent *Arrow*-debate opponents, including both Cobden and his seconder, Milner Gibson, were swept away. Once back in office, Palmerston despatched Lord Elgin to China as plenipotentiary (replacing Bowring, although he remained governor of Hong Kong) with instructions to bring the Chinese to heel. Remarkably, even Elgin acknowledged that the *Arrow* incident was 'a scandal ... and is so considered, I have reason to know, by all except those few personally compromised'. He considered that there was nothing 'more contemptible than the origin of our existing quarrel'. This was not to stop him waging not one, but two bloody colonial wars against the Chinese.

The Second Opium War was little more than an extended technological massacre. As Cobden wrote to Henry Richard of the Peace Society on 13 April 1857,

> the Chinese with their bows and arrows and match-locks, and cannon which will not move, and their painted shields and petticoated officers, have no more chance against our Minie rifles, our 13-inch shells of two thousand yards range, our steamboats and our pivot cannon, than the Peruvians had against Cortez and his men-at-arms. It is not war, it is a battue, a massacre, or slaughter, an execution – call it anything but war – which really means a manly encounter where each side has some chance of success or at least of escape from destruction.

The ferocity of this contemporary critique of British colonial wars has also tended to be absent from the general histories of the period. Cobden is remembered for his leadership of the Anti-Corn Law League, while his much longer-lasting opposition to Britain's wars of colonial aggression is forgotten.

Cobden had earlier condemned the Second Burma War, which was staged on a pretext every bit as flimsy as was the Second Opium War: 'I blush for my country, and the very blood in my veins tingled with indignation at the wanton disregard of all justice and decency which our proceedings towards that country exhibited'. At that time, he had called for

> a map, on Mercator's projection, with a red spot printed upon those places by land and sea where we have fought battles since 1688. It would be seen at a glance that we have (unlike any other nation under the sun) been fighting foreign enemies upon every part of the earth's surface excepting our own territory – thus showing that we have been the most warlike and aggressive people that ever existed.

He believed that this state of affairs had come about because the aristocratic regime that had come to power in 'the Glorious Revolution' had successfully perverted 'the combativeness of the English race to its own sinister ends'. He still hoped that in the future 'peace will become allied with the course of democratic freedom'. While the weakness of Cobden's explanation for Britain's propensity for wars of aggression is demonstrated by the fact that the Manchester middle class was to wholeheartedly endorse Palmerston's China policy in May 1857, his actual identification of Victorian Britain as what would today be called a rogue state has been sadly left unexplored. While Britain's colonial wars are treated as peripheral matters in the histories of the period, this is because, as Cobden pointed out, they were fought in other people's countries. The British bombardment of ports and cities is hardly worth noticing in histories of Britain, it was after all such a regular event, but the damage and casualties inflicted, the relationships established, were much more important for the victims of British aggression. The reality is, as Cobden insisted, that the British state was the most predatory in the world at this time, but the way that this colonial aggression was dressed up in the accoutrements of Liberalism, has effectively disguised this. British militarism and colonial aggression actually presents itself as the 'Pax Britannica'.

Cobden was worried about the effect these wars were having on British national character. On 14 January 1858, soon after the fall of Canton, he wrote to Henry Richard:

> Can we play the game of fraud, violence and injustice in Asia without finding our national conscience seared at home? ... In fact is not our national character already changed? ... Observe the eager levity with which The Times correspondent at Hong Kong is urging on the fray, calling for 'the opening of the ball' ... In due time we shall hear of our forces having at a safe distance with their superior artillery bombarded or burned the crowded city or terrified the population into submission. And all this in support of a quarrel into which our vain and foolish representative plunged us without title of right or reason.

He wondered whether like 'the Romans at the Amphitheatre', the British people had acquired 'a habit of enjoying scenes of carnage, the only difference being that we look at them through the columns of a newspaper'. He feared that it was 'just possible that we may bring on ourselves a retribution from the East by our consistent course of violence and injustice, and God help us if it is to be commensurate with our deserts'.

Before leaving the Second Opium War, it is worth considering, at least briefly, the Great Indian Rebellion with which it overlapped. The troop reinforcements that were despatched to assist Lord Elgin in his China campaign had to be diverted to India to help suppress the outbreak. This was the most serious revolutionary challenge that the British Empire faced in the nineteenth century. Here, in Karl Marx's words, we see all the 'profound hypocrisy and inherent barbarism of bourgeois civilization ... unveiled before our eyes, turning from its home, where it assumes respectable forms, to the colonies where it goes naked'. The Indian Rebellion was put down by means of massacre, torture and pillage on a horrific scale. The historian Michael Edwardes has argued that in this conflict, 'the English threw aside the mask of civilization and engaged in a war of such ferocity that a reasonable parallel can be seen in our times with the Nazi occupation of Europe'. This is not an exaggeration. The most fearful crimes were committed with the full support of both Houses of Parliament. While the massacre of British civilians at Kanpur was cited as justification for British ferocity, the fact is that British atrocities began before this episode and, moreover, almost certainly played a part in provoking it. And, of course, the horrors of Kanpur were completely dwarfed by the horrors that accompanied the sack of Delhi and Lucknow by British troops.

As far as Richard Cobden and his fellow-thinkers were concerned, the Rebellion had been provoked by British aggression. While the cartridges issue might have sparked off mutiny, it was the British annexation of Awadh, a friendly, allied state, in 1856, that turned this into a full-scale rebellion. According to John Bright MP, Cobden's closest political ally, Britain had 'seized a considerable kingdom in India, with which our Government had but recently entered into the most solemn treaty, which every lawyer in England and Europe, I believe, would consider binding before God and the world'. The forcible annexation of this friendly state amounted to 'a great immorality and a great crime, and we have reaped an almost instantaneous retribution in the most gigantic and sanguinary revolt which probably any nation ever made against its conquerors'.

The atrocity stories that circulated among the British community in India and back home in Britain, stories of the rebels raping British women prisoners in public, of women blinded, their noses and ears cut off, forced to watch the torture of their children and even to eat their cooked bodies, made any public expression of sympathy, let alone support for the Rebellion, extremely dangerous. The fact that the atrocity stories were later admitted to be completely untrue did not, of course, lessen their potency at the time. While British prisoners including women and children were killed by the rebels, there had been no rape, torture or mutilation. The stories were fabrications, but they served their purpose, provoking the British troops into ferocious reprisals and justifying those reprisals to British public opinion at home. Cobden, even though he privately confessed that if he were an Indian, he would be 'one of the rebels', nevertheless felt discretion to be the better part of valour. He swallowed many of the atrocity stories in circulation, but still admitted to being appalled by British conduct. He wrote to John Bright on 22 September 1857 that,

> We seem to be in danger of forgetting our own Christianity and descending to a level with these monsters who have startled the world with their deeds. It is terrible to see our middle class journals and speakers calling for the destruction of Delhi, and the indiscriminate massacre of prisoners. To read the letters of our own officers at the commencement of the outbreak, it seemed as if every subaltern had the power to hang or shoot as many natives as he pleased, and they spoke of the work of blood as if they were hunting animals.

Although he condemned rebel atrocities, Cobden still felt their revolt was a response to injustice and oppression. Indeed, he informed another radical colleague, Joseph Sturge, on 31 August 1857, that as far as he was concerned, 'Hindustan must be ruled by those who live on that side of the globe'.

One last point is worth making here: Cobden, a middle-class radical and peace activist, came to despair of any appeal to justice or morality ever moderating the rapacity of the British Empire. Instead, he took comfort from evidence that British aggression was beginning to meet with sterner resistance. He wrote to Henry Richard on 6

November, following a British naval bombardment of Kagoshima in Japan, that he was pleased to say that the engagement, 'judging by the number of killed and wounded on our side', seemed to be 'a drawn battle'. 'I venture to say, with shame', he wrote, 'that this evidence of courage and resources will do more than any appeals to our justice in making us respect the rights of that people in the future'. As countries like Japan and China acquired weapons 'equal to our own ... it may not be in our power to indulge in bloodshed and rapine at so cheap a price'. Resistance, Cobden had reluctantly come to recognize, was the only curb on British Imperial ambitions.

'An English Liberal Government in Revolt Against Liberalism'

This brings us to our second episode, the British invasion of Egypt of 1882, an aggression all the more remarkable because it was carried out by a party only recently elected to office on the basis of its passionate opposition to such colonial adventures. Such reversals are hardly rare in British politics, but this is still a pretty astonishing turnaround. Historians are, of course, especially adept at coping with this sort of thing, and it is safe to say that the unprovoked invasion of Egypt, with its 'vast numbers of Egyptian dead', has barely left a mark on the reputation of the Prime Minister of the day, the great Liberal leader, William Gladstone.

In the autumn of 1879, Gladstone had carried out his celebrated Midlothian campaign, speaking at a succession of mass meetings in Scotland, rallying the Liberal and Radical rank and file, with a tremendous assault on, among other things, the imperial adventures engaged in by Lord Beaconsfield's Conservative government. He was particularly scathing with regard to the government's 'most wanton invasion of Afghanistan', which he proclaimed had 'broken that country in pieces, made it a miserable ruin, destroyed whatever there was in it of peace and order, caused it to be added to the anarchies of the Eastern world'. At another meeting (and remember at this time his speeches were fully reported in the national press), Gladstone told his audience of Afghan villages burned down in reprisal for attacks on British troops. 'Have you ever reflected on the meaning of these words?' he asked. 'The meaning of the burning of the village is that the women and the children were driven forth to perish in the snows of winter'. He called on the British people to remember 'that the sanctity of life in the hill villages of Afghanistan among the winter snows is as inviolable in the eye of Almighty God as can be your own'. Gladstone also condemned in passing, on a number of occasions, another Conservative Imperial initiative, 'our assumption of the virtual government of Egypt'. It is, of course, a great pity that his powerful phrases, delivered with such passion, were so quickly forgotten once in power. Nevertheless, they served their purpose. The Midlothian campaign helped the Liberals to a crushing victory in the General Election of April 1880. They were returned to power with 351 seats and the Conservatives were reduced to 239. Gladstone formed his second government.

The 'virtual government of Egypt' of which Gladstone had complained was a product of that country's bankruptcy. In an attempt to modernize Egypt, the Khedive Ismail had accumulated a huge burden of foreign debt, much of it contracted on terms that were extortionate, passing over into the fraudulent. In 1876, he had announced his intention of postponing interest payments on his loans, only for the British and French governments, acting for the international bondholders, who had bought into the debt, to intervene and take effective control of the Egyptian state. This European control was consolidated in 1878 with the installation of an Englishman, Rivers Wilson, as Minister of Finance, and of a Frenchman, De Blignieres, as Minister of Public Works. To all intents and purposes, the Egyptian government was now serving the interests of the bondholders with the country being run to ensure that the interest on the debt, the bondholders' coupon, was paid. Interestingly, one of the principal architects of this 'virtual government' was a senior Liberal politician, George Goschen, MP for the City of London and the bondholders' representative. Quite coincidentally, he was also the personal financial adviser to one particular bondholder, William Gladstone.

Ismail never accepted the European takeover of his government and did everything in his power to undermine it, even covertly encouraging popular opposition. As early as February 1878, Goschen was confiding to his diary that he might have to be 'deposed if he won't give way'. The following year, Ismail's obstructionism actually led to the Conservative government actually lamenting that it had not got the troops available to invade the country and depose him because of the 'inopportune invasion of Zululand' it was already committed to. Instead of a military occupation, however, the British succeeded in having him removed in a palace *coup d'état*. His compliant son, Tewfik, was installed as a puppet ruler, completely dependent on the British and the French, in June 1879.

Removing Ismail did not solve the problems that confronted the country's 'virtual government'. The exactions of the bondholders were provoking increasing unrest among all sections of Egyptian society, an unrest that more and more took on an Islamic coloration. The government and administration was increasingly filled with European officials, paid considerably more than Egyptian officials and, just as important, paid regularly. Moreover, there was a widespread belief that this was all merely a preliminary before the country was taken over altogether, and incorporated into either the British or the French Empire. One important point worth noting is that the Islamic opposition to European control in Egypt was a modernizing Islam. It demanded, among other things, that the Chamber of Notables, a representative body that had been kept powerless by Ismail, should be given control of the budget, which would have inevitably given it control of the government. Instead of the Khedive being a puppet of the British and the French, he should become a constitutional monarch, presiding over an Egyptian government that was responsible to the Chamber. These demands were supported by the Egyptian Army, which had effectively thrown off Khedival control and under Colonel Ahmed Urabi, placed itself at the disposal of the Chamber. In September 1881, Tewfik was forced by the military to appoint a nationalist government, acceptable to the Chamber. Astonishing as it might seem, the Liberal government's invasion of Egypt in 1882 was precisely to put a stop to these beginnings of representative government and to instead sustain in power the puppet autocracy of the Khedive. The reason was quite simple: any kind of representative government could not be relied on to put the bondholders' interests first, whereas a puppet autocracy, completely dependent on the West for its very existence, could be. There is something very modern about all this.

The Egyptian nationalists, using Wilfred Scawen Blunt, an Arabist and anti-imperialist, as an intermediary, appealed to Gladstone for support. They made clear that they had no intention of repudiating the Egyptian debt and that interest would continue to be paid. What they insisted on, however, was that the Chamber should control the rest of the state's revenues – that is, the small portion that remained once the interest was paid. This was not acceptable. As far as the British were concerned the interests of the bondholders were not compatible with constitutional government. On 8 January 1882, the British and French governments issued a Joint Note making clear their support for Khedival autocracy. Once it became clear that the nationalists would not back down, military intervention became inevitable.

The British Consul-General in Cairo, Sir Edward Malet, made clear what was at stake. He complained on 11 January 1882 that 'the Egyptians have distinctly, for good or evil, entered on a constitutional path'. Nothing could persuade them to abandon this course, so that it was clear that the Chamber would have to be closed down 'forcibly'. With the Egyptian Army supporting the Chamber, this could 'only be done with intervention'. Gladstone's Liberal government was casting itself in the role of Charles I in his conflict with the English Parliament. After a meeting with the President of the Chamber, Mohammad Sultan, in January 1882, Malet wrote to the Foreign Secretary, Lord Granville, that he had informed him 'that our Governments could not consent to the Budget being voted on by the chamber as it would be an infringement of international agreements'. When the President refused to back down, Malet warned him that he risked the same fate as Revolutionary France, 'inundated with the blood of its citizens' and its government overthrown 'by an European coalition against it'. He could still confess to Granville to 'having a repugnance to a war engaged in on behalf of bondholding and which would have for effect to repress the first attempt of a Mussalman country at a Parliamentary Government. It seemed unnatural for England to do this'. The adoption of this particularly reactionary policy is really so remarkable that it is difficult to understand why the histories of the period do not make more of it: a Liberal government using military force to prevent the development of constitutional government in Egypt, the first such development in any Muslim country, in order to ensure that the bondholders received their interest. This tells us so much about the British Empire, indeed, arguably, it tells us too much, so the episode is marginalized or portrayed as something else.

In May 1882, an Anglo-French naval force was despatched to Alexandria in an attempt to intimidate the Egyptians. At the same time, Tewfik was being urged to dismiss the nationalist government, appoint one acceptable to the bondholders and arrest Urabi. His half-hearted attempt at compliance collapsed in the face of popular resistance, and he quickly reinstated the nationlists. Popular outrage at Western arrogance and bullying, nevertheless manifested itself on the streets of Alexandria on 11 June when anti-European rioting broke out. By the time order was restored some 50 Europeans and 250 Egyptians had been killed. The rioting was widely regarded in Britain as a challenge: a native population had laid hands on white men, something that could not possibly be left unpunished. If there was no response Britons would find themselves in danger throughout the Empire and beyond. Moreover, the rioting was widely portrayed as a Muslim attack on Christians. Sir Charles Dilke, a junior member of Gladstone's government, noted in his diary: 'our side in the Commons are very jingo about Egypt. They badly want to kill someone. They don't know who.'

What was needed was a pretext to inflict the necessary punishment and, at the same time, put a stop to all of this nationalist nonsense. The government fastened on the improvements the Egyptians were making to their coastal forts at Alexandria. Despite the fact, privately acknowledged by the Admiralty, that these constituted no threat whatsoever, the British demanded first that the improvements stop, then that the forts be disarmed and lastly that they actually be surrendered to the British. All this, on the grounds of self-defence! Not only was any Egyptian threat non-existent but the British were effectively denying them the right to have any defences. The Egyptians agreed to suspend their improvements, but refused to hand over the forts. On 11 July 1882, the Royal Navy (the French refused to take part in the attack) began a ten-hour bombardment that silenced the forts and left much of Alexandria a smoking ruin. Egyptian casualties were estimated at some 2,000 killed and wounded, while the British had five men killed, and these only because of the degree of contempt in which the British held the Egyptian defences. Subsequently, the British government tried to claim that the Egyptians had burned down Alexandria themselves, but there were numerous British observers at the scene who testified that this was a lie. One example will suffice: the future Admiral, Percy Scott, was sent to recover unexploded shells from the city, including some weighing in at 2,000lbs. British gunnery, he recalled, 'had not been very good, and the town appeared to me to have suffered more from the misses than the forts had from the hits'. Back at the House of Commons, Dilke observed that 'our Jingo gang' was all very excited by news of the slaughter. The bombardment of Alexandria, he noted, 'like all butchery is popular'.

The bombardment only produced one resignation from this government elected to oppose colonial adventures. The veteran radical, John Bright, the friend and colleague of the late Richard Cobden, felt that he could not be a party to action 'which I deem unjust and unnecessary'. He had been growing increasingly concerned at 'how much of the Jingo or war spirit can be shown by certain members of a Liberal Cabinet'. He wrote to Lord Ripon that if he had not resigned, 'my whole political life would have been stained beyond recovery ... That the war began in self-defence is absurd'. Gladstone's efforts at persuading him to stay were, to say the least, unconvincing. He argued that the bombardment of Alexandria had 'shown the fanaticism of the East that the massacre of Europeans is not likely to be perpetrated with impunity', and, moreover, it had 'greatly advanced the Egyptian question towards a permanent and peaceable solution'. Gladstone assured Bright with complete sincerity that 'I feel that in being a party to this work I have been a labourer in the cause of peace'. While Bright considered 'the Egyptian incident rather as a deplorable blunder than as a crime', nevertheless it was only in this that it differed 'from the worst doings of Palmerston'. On the day he resigned Bright wrote an assessment of Gladstone in his diary:

> He seems to have the power of convincing himself that what to me seems a glaring wrong is evidently right, and though he regrets that a crowd of men should be killed, he regards it almost as an occurrence which is not to be condemned, as if it was one of the incidents of a policy out of which he hopes for a better order of things. He even spoke of our being able to justify our conduct in the great day of account.

Gladstone, as many of his contemporaries complained, could convince himself of the moral correctness of just about anything.

The bombardment of Alexandria did not overthrow the nationalists and restore Tewfik to power. Instead, the British had to despatch an expeditionary force under General Sir Garnett Wolseley to conquer and occupy the country. This obviously could not be presented to British public opinion as a war for the benefit of the bondholders. Instead, it was presented as a war of liberation undertaken to free the Egyptians from a military dictatorship. The suppression of the Chamber disappeared from the agenda and the removal of Urabi took its place as being more congenial. The architects of this particular justification for the invasion were Sir Charles Dilke and Joseph Chamberlain. Dilke made clear on one occasion that a public despatch recounting developments actually made it seem that 'Urabi was the man of the Chamber and that the Chamber fights on reasonable grounds'. The despatch showed Urabi as a 'patriot' and Dilke insisted that it be redrafted with a different 'spin' so that everything 'telling against him ought to be put in the despatch'. It was Chamberlain, however, who persuaded the Cabinet that the invasion should be presented not as an attempt 'to impose on Egypt institutions of our choice but to secure for the Egyptian people a free choice for themselves so far as this may not be inconsistent with the permanent interests of other Powers'. In the Commons, Chamberlain actually proclaimed that Egypt was being invaded and large numbers of Egyptians were being slaughtered as a way of 'liberating the national sentiment' in the country. He was, of course, lying through his teeth, dressing up a reactionary war as something progressive, proclaiming that a war fought for the bondholders was, in fact, a war fought for the Egyptian people. This was dishonesty on an historic scale, and, once again, seems remarkably contemporary. These 'convenient theories', as Bernard Holland observed some 30 years later, 'liberalized armed intervention'.

When the war came to be voted on in the Commons, it was carried by 275 votes to 21. The spirit of Midlothian was well and truly dead. The 'peace party' in the Commons collapsed in the face of Gladstone's turnaround. Confronted with the choice of peace or Gladstone, MPs who would have been fierce, uncompromising opponents of any Tory invasion, rallied with varying degrees of enthusiasm in support of a Liberal invasion. Even the Peace Society, that had for so long been an opponent of British colonial adventures, broke under the strain. Its president, J. W. Pease, abstained in the vote, but the Society's two vice-presidents voted for the invasion. Not one Quaker MP voted against, something without precedent, and once again entirely due to the fact that it was Gladstone who was the aggressor. The Anti-Aggression League that had been formed by Frederic Harrison and Herbert Spencer, and which numbered over thirty Liberal MPs among its members, turned out, as Harrison bitterly observed to be the 'Anti-Tory Aggression League'. Its parliamentary membership 'slid decorously and with elaborate justifications into a somewhat apologetic Imperialism' and voted overwhelmingly for war. The opposition in the Commons was provided, in the main, by the Irish Nationalists. There was more opposition outside Parliament, but even here many of those who would have been vocal in their opposition to a Tory war remained silent in the face of Gladstone's war.

The Egyptian Army was routed at the battle of Tel-el-Kebir on 13 September 1882. The Egyptians were overwhelmed in a surprise attack that had all the characteristics of a well-executed colonial massacre. The British had 57 men killed and 382 wounded. The number of Egyptian dead was, as is the way with colonial wars, not actually counted, but estimates range from 2,000 to 10,000. One British officer, Colonel William Butler, was to ask in his memoirs whether the war was a matter of 'the Egyptian peasant in revolt against his plunderers or an English Liberal government in revolt against Liberalism'. This was, he felt, the sort of war 'which the Stock Exchange is now able to bestow'. It was, he told his wife, the celebrated war artist, Elizabeth Butler, 'not a matter for exultation' to 'beat those poor fellaheen soldiers'. Many of the actual participants felt that there was little glory in such an unequal contest.

Gladstone, however, was jubilant. He was determined to capitalize on the success and wanted the guns fired in celebration in Hyde Park and church bells rung throughout the land. As for Urabi, he hoped that he could be speedily hanged, a sentiment shared by Queen Victoria. When the conquering army returned home, the government staged a triumphant celebration that proved, according to one contemporary observer, 'how popular any war is, or any successful war'. The peace movement could preach all it wanted, but it could not preach out of the soul of an Englishman his passion for war. And, of course, the bondholders profited handsomely from the war, because not only were their interest payments safeguarded, but their investments in the Egyptian debt appreciated in value once the country had been occupied. Gladstone was, of course, one of these beneficiaries and, given how popular the Egyptian debt was with investors, it is safe to assume so were many other MPs, both Liberals and Conservatives. Nevertheless, Gladstone could still stand up in front of a meeting in Wales on 3 October, less than a month after the slaughter at Tel-el-Kebir, and tell his audience in all sincerity that 'We have carried out this war from a love of peace'.

Between 1882 and 1922, successive British governments were to make no less than 66 official declarations of their intention to withdraw from Egypt. In the event, British troops were to remain until they were forced out at the end of 1954. Indeed, they were so fond of the country that they invaded it again in 1956. Even though over 70 years had passed since Gladstone's invasion, Anthony Eden's Conservative government went ahead and invented a fraudulent pretext for the invasion of Egypt as if nothing had changed in all that time. On this occasion, the pretext was particularly shameful even by the dubious standards set by the British Empire for the justification of attacks on weaker countries. Eden made the likes of Palmerston, Gladstone and Chamberlain look like men of honour, paragons of integrity.

The British secretly conspired with the French and the Israelis to launch an unprovoked attack on the Egyptians. All three countries had causes for their aggression: the British saw the Egyptian nationalization of the Suez Canal as threatening their position throughout the Middle East, the French objected to Egyptian support for the great Algerian revolt, and the Israelis had expansionist ambitions with regard to all their neighbours. What they decided, however, was that while the Israelis would launch an unprovoked surprise attack, the British and the French would come to their aid under the guise of peacekeeping. Once the Israelis had invaded, the two governments would issue an ultimatum that both sides should evacuate the Suez Canal area. This, it was known, would be completely unacceptable to the Egyptians who would have to retreat to comply while the Israelis would be able to advance. When, as predicted, the Egyptians rejected the ultimatum, Britain and France joined in the attack, bombing Egyptian positions and invading at Suez.

The Suez invasion is probably the single most dishonest action of any British government in modern times. The enormity of the attempted deception still takes the breath away, an unprovoked aggression under the guise of peacekeeping, this is prize-winning stuff. The trouble was that it never actually deceived anyone. And, moreover, the United States that was in the process of replacing British influence in the Middle East, used its economic and political power to force a humiliating withdrawal. While Eden subsequently resigned, one of the other architects of this great deception, Harold Macmillan, succeeded him as Prime Minister, and even after such a dreadful fiasco, the Conservatives still remained in office until 1964.

From Palmerston to Blair

One thing is clear from the history we have examined. It is that there is absolutely no incompatibility between constitutional government and colonial aggression. Moreover, this remains true once we arrive at the post-1918 period with its democratic franchise. The Suez invasion of 1956, despite considerable domestic opposition, although it has to be said that the stance of the Labour front bench was opportunistic rather than principled, failed because of the intervention of the United States. And, of course, the Conservative Party responsible for the fiasco went on to win the 1959 General Election. It is also worth remembering that one of the most appalling episodes of colonial repression in British history, the brutal suppression of the Mau Mau rebellion in Kenya, occurred in the 1950s. Between 1952 and 1960, over a thousand rebels were hanged, including 472 for the possession of firearms, many of them home-made, and an incredible 62 were hanged for the administration of illegal oaths. This, remember, was the 1950s, not the 1250s or the 1550s. The torture of suspects was routine, and prisoners were regularly shot out of hand. The Conservative governments of the day covered up the most terrible atrocities, and only a handful of those responsible were ever prosecuted, receiving derisory punishments that amounted to official condoning of the offences. There was remarkably little popular opposition to the repression in Kenya, especially considering its downright savagery.

More recently, we have seen Tony Blair's New Labour Government resorting to a stratagem of invented pretexts that would have been familiar to Palmerston and Bowring, Chamberlain and Gladstone, in order to justify participation in the United States' invasion of Iraq. While the pretext was the threat posed by Iraq's fictional weapons of mass destruction (and in the United States by the equally fictional links between Saddam Hussein and al-Qaeda), the actual objective was to establish American Imperial domination over the Middle East, a domination in which Britain hoped to be a junior partner. By 2003, however, things had changed. New Labour was confronted by a massive, indeed, an unprecedented anti-war movement, the Stop The War Coalition. Remarkable as it still seems, the largest demonstration in British history, the 2,000,000-strong, 15 February 2003 demonstration, was against a Labour government's plans for an unprovoked and illegal aggression. It is a testament to how successfully Blair and his supporters have been in transforming the Labour Party that they were able to go to war regardless. In retrospect, it seems that Blair was confident that no matter how flimsy his 'weapons of mass destruction' pretext might be, once the war had begun, public opinion would rally round. And, once the war was won, a foregone conclusion as Iraq was virtually defenceless in the face of American military might and certainly had no weapons of mass destruction, a victorious war would prove a popular war. As Sir Charles Dilke put it in 1882, 'all butchery is popular'.

This is no longer the case. Indeed, as the invasion of Iraq has turned into a protracted catastrophe, particularly for the Iraqi people themselves, so the New Labour government has had to invent new pretexts for the invasion. The invasion has subsequently been portrayed as the liberation of the Iraqi people from tyranny and more recently as a front in 'the war on terror'. Neither of these claims should be taken seriously. Firstly, both the British and the United States governments have no problem maintaining good, indeed, close relations with tyrannies, as long as they do what the United States wants. If they are prepared to fit into the United States' New World Order, then their internal regime is not an issue. A good demonstration of this is provided by American hostility to Iran, which defies US power, but which has a parliamentary system, however imperfect, and American friendship with Saudi Arabia, which is an undisguised autocracy that, moreover, practices a form of Islam that makes the Iranian regime, which is reactionary enough, look secular. As for the 'war on terror' which we are promised (or more properly threatened) is going to last for decades, this is an ideological construct, a propaganda fiction, which can be used to justify present and future colonial aggressions, most recently the Israeli attack on Lebanon and most likely a future attack on Iran. It is the ultimate pretext.

All the evidence shows that whatever government is in power it will be able to deliver a compliant majority to endorse whatever might be the next aggression. We are in uncharted waters, however, because for the first time the great majority of the British people stand with the opponents of colonial wars, no matter how they are dressed up or with however much false sincerity they are advocated.

Chapter 4

Chartism – Towards a
New Politics

John Charlton

On Monday 11 October 1819, a reported 100,000 people con-
gregated in Newcastle and marched to the Town Moor for a monster
rally to protest the massacre at Peterloo two months earlier, and to
assert the right to vote. The population of the borough of Newcastle
was just over 30,000. Men, women and children walked for up to
five hours from the towns, villages and countryside, then up to five
hours back. On the basis of the 1820 Census figures for North-
umberland and Durham approximately one in two able-bodied
adults attended. From the press reports in 1819 to the publication of
Edward Thompson's *The Making of the English Working Class* in
1963, the event virtually disappeared from history. Other events in
that agitated autumn suffered a similar fate. In September, as many
as 300,000 turned out in north London to welcome the main speaker
at Manchester, Henry Hunt. Newcastle's meeting was the biggest
outside of London but in that autumn mass meetings were held in
Birmingham, Nottingham, Preston, Halifax, Bradford, Carlisle,
Glasgow and many other places.

In the British constitution, changes in law are only registered in
parliamentary acts. In the contemporary record and in the writing of
history the minutiae of parliamentary proceedings, and the behaviour and thoughts of its major and minor participants, are widely
reported and usually readily available to posterity. What happens
beyond Westminster may be underplayed, distorted or ignored.
Seeking out and grappling with the fragmentary evidence of the

latter is the responsibility of those wishing to establish a more rounded account.

Take the Newcastle reform meeting. It sparked a parliamentary debate. More precisely, its detail was a central part of the debate on the aftermath of Peterloo. Lord Darlington saw in it evidence of a wide conspiracy of the lower orders to violently seize the property of the landed. There were some dissenters from this view, most articulately the MP for Newcastle, Matthew White Ridley, but the consensus followed Lord Darlington. Parliament was peopled overwhelmingly by middle-aged and elderly men of the landed interest. In 1819, a Member aged 50 would have been reared against the background of the French Revolution, the terror and two decades of war with France. French aristocratic survivors of those events were part of social life. For the ruling class, 'Jacobinism' was a word with a similar resonance to 'communism' in the USA in the 1950s.

Recently, however, a new home-grown 'terror' had begun to trouble the minds of the rulers. In 1812, machine breakers had appeared in Yorkshire, Lancashire and the Midlands. The Luddites struggled to resist the consequences of the headlong rush into technological innovation within a laissez-faire economic system. In 1815, the seamen manning the coal trade picketed the mouths of the rivers Tyne, Wear and Blyth for six weeks, bringing the business to a complete halt. In Manchester in 1818, cotton-mill workers struck using the new strategy of flying pickets to close the trade. And, during the month of the Newcastle reform demonstration, the keelmen on the Tyne closed down the coal trade for three weeks. If the Luddites were to some extent part of the older industrial world of the domestic system, the strikers, open, belligerent, and above all, well organized, despite the legal restrictions on combination, were harbingers of a new phenomenon: open class struggle.

In the 30 or so years which followed Peterloo, class struggle was at the heart of the growing debate over reform. Though it appeared to be fought out in the arcane world of the Houses of Parliament, the context was rapid change in society: the assertion of the trade cycle, industrialization and urbanization. The reform movement inside and outside of Parliament ebbed and flowed throughout this period

– it peaked in 1819 outside of Parliament. Against a background of economic turbulence, the most radical activists saw a widened suffrage as an essential pre-requisite to improve the situation of the poor and destitute. Committees were formed and meetings were held in many parts of the country, at their strongest in London and the industrial areas. The meeting in Manchester in August which resulted in Peterloo was one such. The anger released by the event provoked the spread of the movement, fuelled by the unbending response of the government and judiciary. The refusal of the authorities to yield to the demand for an enquiry was followed by the enactment of further repressive legislation, the deployment of troops, arrests and the conviction of radical organizers and journalists. The arrest, trial and execution of the Cato Street conspirators in 1820 brought a temporary slackening of radical activity in London and the country.

Twelve months later the movement regrouped, especially in London. In the winter of 1820, George III died. His son and successor George IV was deeply unpopular. His wife, Queen Caroline, badly maltreated by the King and the government became a focus for renewed activity and one which had support in Parliament. The scale of protest was considerable, with repeated street protest organized by the London artisans, reaching beyond her premature death to her funeral procession in 1821. It was an improbable issue for a radical movement. In fact, it was an effective means of hitting the government and reviving a movement battered by repressive legislation. The crowds in the streets simply defied the old and new laws forbidding assemblies for political purposes. The government was weakened. Two of the key architects of repression over the past decade, Sidmouth and Castlereagh, castigated in Shelley's poem, *The Mask of Anarchy* (1819), were both gone inside a year. The third was Prime Minister Liverpool who then presided over a divided and weak administration.

In 1824, in a remarkable reversal for reaction, the Combination Acts passed at the height of the French Wars in 1799–1800, were repealed after a short campaign orchestrated by Francis Place, a small number of radical employers and a few MPs. The radical press, apparently severely handicapped by arrests under the Six Acts of 1819, virtually ignored the law during the Queen Caroline Affair, carrying their agitation straight into the repeal campaign. Economic revival brought new confidence to workers and trade unionism came out of the shadows for the first time in thirty years but in a very different world from the 1780s. Industrialization had moved a long way in that time. There were many more factories and workshops. Some were quite large, numbering their workforce in hundreds rather than tens. It was a more favourable situation for trade unionism. Of course, employers hardly welcomed this, attributing the upsurge in activity to changes in the law. Attempts to reverse repeal were warded off, and the right to establish a union was established. However, there was still plenty of law on the statute book as the men of Tolpuddle were to discover in 1834. Nonetheless, economic buoyancy made the mid-1820s a relatively safe time for trade union activity.

Economic downturn returned after 1826. Unemployment rose, and militant activity fell away. At the same time, there was a crisis in the political elite which was adjusting unevenly to laissez faire economics. Sections of business wanted to modify the restrictions imposed by the Navigation Acts, and there was controversy over the price of corn imposed in the Corn Laws. Then there were restrictions on the rights of both Roman Catholics and Free Church Protestants. Neither group could any longer be truly regarded as endangering the state. The Stuart cause was completely dead, and a Catholic middle class in Ireland could even be seen as a force for stability. Large sections of the 'new' middle class in England embraced Methodism, Quakerism and other non-conformist sects. By the 1820s, a repeal of the Test and Corporation Acts permitting non-Anglicans to hold office was conceded. At the end of the decade, after stirrings in Ireland and the election of the Catholic Daniel O'Connell twice, the most obdurate anti-papists were overruled in Parliament. However, one consequence actually fuelled the broader demand for parliamentary reform. In order to restrict the numbers of Catholics qualifying for the property vote in Irish elections, Parliament raised the property qualification, and disqualified hundreds of Protestant voters who had earlier been included as a means of reinforcing Orange authority in the wake of the 1798 rebellion.

The somewhat more open nature of political life in the 1820s, removed from the memories of war and its awful economic aftermath, fostered enquiry and debate beyond society's elites. There was almost a frenzy of interest in workers' education. Founding meetings of the Mechanics Institutes could attract thousands of workers. These institutions developed like a rash in the decade as groups were formed in towns and villages across Britain. Middle-class radicals and advanced employers were usually the initiators, and they had their own agendas including the domesticating of working men. Nevertheless, the Institutes played an important part in developing literacy and a sense of collectivity. But they were merely part of a process which Edward Thompson called warrening society. Artisans joined literary and philosophical societies, political and trades clubs and cooperative initiatives. The decade was a significant moment in the development of political and social theories as the sharpest intellects struggled to explain the flood-tide of change within which they were embroiled.

Broadening education achieved in the comparative freedom of the mid-1820s became a vital part of the political process in the more intense times ushered in at the end of the decade. Economic downturn and the return of unemployment turned the masses back towards the necessity for political reform. Employers were only too ready to attempt to wrestle back the gains made by working people. Class antagonism sharpened. The explosion of revolutionary sentiment in Europe in 1830 fanned the flame. There was a strong fear that the Duke of Wellington and his supporters would attempt to go to the help of the reactionary regime of Charles X in France. Whigs tried to head off rising popular anger with the demand for parliamentary reform.

Some, and especially those in Parliament, saw modest reform as crucial to protecting property from the possibility of revolutionary upsurge. Their aim was to bring the unfranchised prosperous middle class into the pale of the parliamentary system in the hope of building a coalition for the status quo. In a borough like Newcastle, where such men already had the vote as freemen of the town, they were usually a conservative force which regularly returned both moderate Whig and Tory members to parliament.

In parliamentary terms, political reform was by no means guaranteed. Despite the absurdities of the existing system it was not only the most reactionary elements that feared that even modest concessions could create an insatiable appetite for change. This anxious response against a background of rural disturbance and urban revolt blocked the first modest Whig proposals in 1831. There were sharp antagonisms within the Tory governing coalition. Some were irreconcilable in the short term, especially the rearguard action of protectionism against the drive of free market capitalism, clearly expressed in differences over the Corn Laws. But these sides were also cross cut by differences over Catholic emancipation, treatment of the poor, and factory conditions. Wellington was unable to hold the line. In some ways the arrival in Downing Street of Earl Grey, a moderate reformer since the 1780s, was the last card of the old regime. His 'not so great reform bill', as Paul Foot called it, succeeded in just about binding enough of the middle class into his project to outmanoeuvre the radicalism of the streets expressed most dramatically in major insurgency in Merthyr, Bristol and Nottingham but universally in mass meetings and in a plethora of political clubs and radical publications which defied the remorseless curbs on press freedom. The 'great betrayal' brought smug triumphalism in governing circles but much bitterness on the streets and taverns where radicals met.

The former was a fuel for the Poor Law Commission Report, and the establishment of the attempt to abandon outdoor relief in favour of the physical and psycho-brutality of the workhouse. The hubris implicit in the notion that minute reforms had produced a 'perfect system' perhaps also encouraged the judges who transported the men of Tolpuddle in 1834, and the Glasgow Cotton spinners in 1837. The relentless drive accelerated in the decade to reorganize the labour process at enormous cost to the livelihood of armies of outworkers in the textile and metal industries.

Fierce and unrelenting as the repression was the popular end of the radical movement was just not intimidated. Craftsmen's societies flourished. Great experiments were mounted to unionize the unskilled, though with limited success. Political societies were hot-beds of discussion of political economy among workers. Particular anger focused on the Poor Law Commission and the savage perse-cution of trade unionists. The blatant class attitudes of the rulers helped to nurture a sense of class, contributing to a renewed understanding of the need for political power. Out of this came Chartism.

Formally, the Chartist movement was born among the craftsmen of London who published a pamphlet, *The Rotten House of Common* in 1836, a mocking attack on the 'fraudulent' reform measures of 1832. A few months later, at the Crown and Anchor pub, a petition was issued laying out a case arguing that laws could only be legit-imate if those called upon to obey them had played a part in drafting them through their representatives in parliament. It was not a new idea. It mirrored the American Declaration of Independence of 1776 and indeed the Putney Debates of 200 years earlier. The germ of this idea was a continuing part of English radical tradition. What made its reappearance different in the 1830s was a social force, the working class, with the potential to bring about wide-ranging change. The petition codified the idea round a series of Six Points, *The People's Charter*.

Of the six points the most important was most certainly, 'uni-versal manhood suffrage'. It was important for two opposing rea-sons. It had the capacity to unite everyone except the tiny property-owning minority who already enjoyed the right to vote. That tiny minority saw it as a threat to their hold on power, and indeed their property. In the earlier reform agitation this minority had not been united. The issues were not represented quite so starkly since a sizeable part of the middle class had no vote, but much more to the point the seats of bourgeois power, the industrial town, were hardly represented at all. Redistribution of seats had redressed that situa-tion to a degree satisfactory to this constituency. The bourgeoisie of Birmingham, Manchester, Leeds and Liverpool had their place at the table. Remaining dissatisfaction was easily held in check, however, by the demand for 'universal manhood suffrage'. Few could judge better than the urban bourgeoisie the likely consequences of such a measure. Not only did they employ the workers but, in the 1830s perhaps most of them still lived in the same districts. Even those who did not see workers at work, like bankers, attorneys, and many men of the cloth, were daily witnesses to the habits and conditions of the proletariat. Ruling-class unity was more or less assured during the Chartist period.

What about the Chartists? Justifying the claim that there was a growing class consciousness needs a very wide-angled perspective. While there were demonstrably moments of mass unity they were few, but the most advanced political activists entering the Chartist campaign came from wide circles and distinctive backgrounds. It was the London artisans who codified the demands in the charter. Among working people in the period they were probably the most highly literate anywhere, with a high sense of self-worth embedded in values and practices shaped over centuries. The sentiment for widening democracy reached back at least into the seventeenth century among 'the middling folk' in the English revolution. The spark for heightened activity probably came from the Reform Act's insult to their self-worth. Like their London counterparts, the Birmingham artisans had been engaged with the reform campaign of the early 1830s, though unlike London the leadership was more obviously middle class. Thomas Atwood, the banker, was untypical of his section of the middle class in not being seduced by Grey and Russell's sleight of hand. Of course, one of the problems with the artisan groups, which probably accounts for their relative con-servatism in Chartist strategies, was the fact that most had their futures bound up with the success of their enterprises. Apprentice, journeyman, small master was still a possible route. Moral force with the petition was the desired strategy, and in the ebbs of the movement a shift into the campaign for educational reform was an outcome. There were exceptions in particularly advanced and determined individuals, and in trades directly threatened by advances in capitalist technology and organization.

Many Lancashire and some Yorkshire textile workers had been factory workers all their lives, and had experienced both the worst excesses and the organizational advantages of factory life. In the mass strike of 1842, Lancashire factory workers, led by self-proclaimed Chartists, were in its vanguard using the mass picket to spread the strike. They had instant success in the factory districts because they were tapping into a commonality of experience where solidarity was already an understood concept. The flying pickets could bring out the workers in small workshops when they crossed the Pennines into West Yorkshire, but solidarity was difficult to sustain when the pickets had passed on, and small masters could appeal to *their* common purpose or just threaten consequences. There is a question of how far the mass strike was a Chartist enterprise given that the entire national leadership either opposed it or distanced themselves entirely from it. Rank and file leaders like Pilling and Hutchinson in Lancashire, and Cooper in the Midlands were clearly Chartists and the authorities were quick to make the association believing that the threat to property implicit in suffrage extension was a convenient stick with which to beat the 43 men, including Feargus O'Connor, who were brought to trial at Lancaster in the wake of the strike. O'Connor had been one of the leaders who distanced himself from the strike, absenting himself from Manchester with haste at the beginning of August 1842.

In the first wave of the struggle in 1839, the vanguards of the movement were colliers and iron workers from South Wales. There, artisan outlooks, if at all significant, were present in the old centres of textile production like Llandiloes a focus for a modest militant upsurge in the spring of 1839. It was easily crushed by the authorities. In South Wales in that autumn the spark for the insurgency was provided by the persecution of Henry Vincent, the Chartist touring lecturer. In the region of 30,000 workers from the mining and iron-working valleys of eastern Wales marched on Newport, where they mistakenly believed Vincent was being held. The coordination of the rising, and the inability of the authorities to find and punish significant numbers of its leaders, suggest both an experienced leadership with a widespread network, and considerable community consent for the action. The leaders who were seized upon were tried and given the ultimate sentence, though this was commuted to transportation.

It may be that this act, the sentences meted out in 1843 and subsequently in 1848 after the third Chartist upsurge, marked a significant change in the thinking of the ruling class. The retreat from the death penalty, previously used in the putting down of the Merthyr Rising of 1831, may have reflected even dimly a coming to terms with the emerging potential power of the working class. Making martyrs might keep issues burning, and might give further opportunities for disturbance. If the death penalty was not viable in 'political' situations, and transportation was the most effective substitute, it would be seen that after John Frost was sent to Tasmania a substantial campaign was mounted and sustained for his release and return. In 1843 and 1848, short prison sentences took the place of transportation. Short sentences were extremely damaging to the victims. The man lost his employment, with serious consequences for his dependants. Deprived of the most articulate and determined organizers, with would-be replacement leaders possibly intimidated, the movement suffered serious set backs. The government of Lord John Russell, the erstwhile reformer, seemed to appreciate the efficacy of such a strategy.

A second important part of the strategy was never to concede that offences were political. The prosecution of editors and newspaper sellers, for example, was always for evading stamp duty rarely for the opinions expressed in the publications, while organizers of trade union activity were charged with conspiracy or some related or similar offence. The manner of applying the law to suppressing the activity of the disfranchised is clear evidence of the growing awareness by the smartest minds in the ruling class of new forces rising in society with industrialization, and that these forces just could not continue to be met by brute force, except as a last resort. This is surely the meaning of the string of measures, including the 1832 settlement, and the 1835 municipal corporations act, both of which sought to win the emerging middle classes to the political and social compact, lighter sentencing to minimize the possibilities of martyrdom, the toleration of trade unionism, and a little later the incremental extension of the franchise to new sections of the population.

At the three high points of activity in 1839, 1842 and 1848 the focus of the most intense activity was regional, South Wales in 1839, Lancashire in 1842 and London in 1848. Nevertheless, in each case there was a national or near national movement in being. In 1839, before Newport, a Chartist convention assembled in London. This was a delegate body with representatives from many places including what were considered centres of radicalism: Newcastle, Glasgow, Bradford, Leeds, Sheffield, Birmingham, Norwich and Bristol. Class composition and the size and content of the meeting were dictated by certain restrictions. The men who travelled from the provinces needed to be of independent means since working men could not leave their work and keep their jobs. Secondly, the existing law forbade assemblies of over fifty. Finally, spies would be expected to be present recording the contributions for the attention of the Home Secretary. These restrictions trammelled an open discussion of strategy and tactics beyond the decision to advance the petition and spread the word through the country by 'missionaries', and the circulation of the recently founded newspaper, the *Northern Star*.

One such missionary was Henry Vincent whose fate became so bound up with the autumn rebellion in South Wales. The other important figures in this first phase were Bronterre O'Brien, William Lovett, Feargus O'Connor, Julian Harney and Peter Murray McDouall. O'Brien and Lovett were both central to the very creation of the movement. The latter was the actual architect of the Six Points. He was a key figure in the London Working Men's Association who believed strongly in education as the major tool in making working people both fit to vote and acceptable to those with the power to change the law. As the movement moved to the streets, and even picked up the gun, his interest cooled and his influence waned.

Bronterre O'Brien, referred to as the 'school master of Chartism', came to the fore during the Reform Bill Crisis, and subsequently in the pages of the popular newspaper *The Poor Man' Guardian*. In issue after issue he dissected the Reform Act, and upbraided its architects and supporters. Most importantly he was one of the first to raise the critical question of whether political democracy was enough given, as he saw it, the tyranny of the workplace. He too was virtually absent from the militant phase of the movement. He may be seen, however, as the most important figure intellectually since after 1848 in the remaining years before the shrinking and disappearance of the movement, O'Brien's ideas were central to the creation of a social democratic platform for the National Charter Association.

The two outstanding figures were certainly O'Connor and Harney. Feargus O'Connor was a flamboyant Irish journalist who had meteorically entered the national political scene by winning an Irish seat in Parliament from which he was twice disqualified. He had the means to found the *Northern Star*, the remarkable weekly paper which at its peak reached a circulation figure of 50,000 copies, and even in the worst days between 1843 and 1848 never fell below 7,000. Its 'readership' was much wider than these figures, since a common practice was to have collective readings in cottages and hostelries. Cogent articles, including masses of readers' contributions, aided the education of its audience, advancing the understanding of the facets of democracy. O'Connor and his young colleague Julian Harney toured the countryside speaking at hundreds of meetings, and helping to build a national organization. Harney was influenced by the ultra democratic and insurrectionary ideas of Gracchus Baboeuf's left Jacobinism in the French Revolution. Despite spells in prison, both these figures remained popular agitators throughout the period, although after 1848 O'Connor suffered bouts of depression and, despite winning the parliamentary seat of Nottingham in 1847, his powers declined. If his first great achievement had been to kindle the fire of Chartism between 1836 and 1843, his second was to hold the movement together in the mid-1840s through the organization of the Land Plan.

Harney was also a fine journalist and orator, who contributed two special ideas to the radical movement even wider and more durable than Chartism. He attempted to bring it closer to trade unionism, a plan he held in common with his mentor O'Brien, but also very significant was the fight to internationalize the movement. He was particularly active in this respect round the events of 1848, seeing the Chartist movement as intimately related to the revolutionary upsurge in that year.

In its early stages, Peter Murray McDouall was another tireless Chartist lecturer speaking at hundreds of meetings, from Scotland to the South West. He had a very well developed sense of class, and of the importance of involving workers in the movement. He spent time on the run from the authorities and was lost at sea in 1854 when migrating to Australia. In its last phase the key figure was Ernest Jones, the son of a gentleman, who tried to shift the movement towards social democracy as being the only way to safeguard any measure of political democracy which might be achieved. He was much debilitated by two years in prison after 1848, but he recovered to play the leading role in the National Charter Association. Unfortunately for him and that new organization, the street radicalism of the spring and summer of 1848 waned rapidly under the twin forces of state repression and improved economic circumstances.

The decline lasted for a decade, almost as long as the growth period. In its early phase it was a mass movement which engaged tens of thousands of lower-middle-class and working-class people furious with the outcome of the reform movement of the early 1830s. This disillusionment was fuelled by the onslaught of the ruling class reflecting the demands of its bourgeois component in repressing trade unionism, and installing a New Poor Law aimed at forcing workers to accept low wages, or to give up their freedom by entering the new bastilles. But, like all mass movements, Chartism was subject to economic cadences, state repression and the vagaries of leadership. Each of these processes was replete with lessons for participants. By 1842 the Jacobin tactic of seizure of power by determined minorities was all but dead. Persuasion by petitioning and large gatherings was similarly a spent force by 1848. Persuasion by education was also discredited. The utopian idea of gathering in likeminded Chartist communities maintained an organizational basis for the movement in difficult times, but was no solution to the deprivation and lack of citizenship of the overwhelming majority of

Britons. After 1848, the movement re-grouped around a set of ideas held earlier by only a few like Bronterre O'Brien. The National Charter Association was also an attempt to put the movement on a stable organizational base, a membership organization with a con-stitution and elected officers. In these respects it pre-figured the socialist parties which emerged 50 years later. State repression, but perhaps more importantly economic revival, which had undone Chartism as a mass movement, turned the determined survivors towards trade unionism, cooperation and personal education. In its final phase, Chartism was a political movement before its time.

Chapter 5

Labourism – What's Left?

David Powell

The memorial in the wall of Burford Church, Oxon, is a modest one, simply listing three good English names: Cornet Thompson, Corporal Perkins, and Private Church. Its very modesty, however, disguises its significance, for it was here, in this quiet English churchyard, that in May 1649, and in defence of the new-found Commonwealth, Cromwell put down a Leveller rising, and executed its ringleaders for declaring in *England's Standard Advanced* that they had marched 'with Swords in our hands to redeem our selves, and the Land of Our Nativity, from slavery and oppression.'

The challenge to power was explicit, an echo of a time long-passed when the recusant priest, John Ball, called on God to intercede in the name of the peasantry for: 'My good people, things can never go well in England, nor never can, until all goods are held in common ... and we shall all be equal' – to be hung, drawn and quartered in 1381 for his presumption; a foretaste of a time when the emergent bourgeoisie of the nineteenth century would mobilize 'the mere people' to campaign for the pseudonymous Great Reform Bill, of which Bertrand Russell, grandson of the Bill's architect, was to write: 'Ever since 1832, the upper classes of England have been faced with retaining as much of the substance of power, whilst abandoning their forms to the clamour of democrats.'

The past may be a good place to visit, but it is no place to stay. And if the sense of betrayal is deep rooted – of promises made, and never kept; of undertakings given and never fulfilled – then it is compounded by the divide that has riven English radicalism: of Cromwell's rejection of the ultra-libertarian's contention that 'the poorest he that is in England hath a life to lead as the greatest he, and therefore, truly, Sir, I think it's clear that every man that is to live under a government ought first by his owne consent, put himself under that government'; of the rancorous contest between the physical and moral force Chartists of the 1840s; of the bitter disputes that divided the nascent Labour Party at the turn of the twentieth century. In each case the ends to be achieved were much the same – the rights to participate as citizens in a democratic society, the rights to due process of law, the rights to a measure of economic equity – it was in the means to achieve them that they differed.

Seemingly the differences were innate, unbridgeable as William Morris, poet and craftsman turned political activist and founder of the Socialist League, learned when he set about 'making Socialists' in the late nineteenth century. Conscious of past betrayals, and contemptuous of Parliament, that 'dung hill' at Westminster, which he had come to regard as little better than a society for the preservation of vested interests, Morris stumped the country declaring a 'holy warfare against the age':

> The real business of Socialists is to impress on the workers the fact that they are a class, whereas they ought to be a Society, if we mix ourselves up with Parliament we shall confuse and dull this fact in people's minds ... If by any chance any good is to be got out of the legislation of the ruling classes, the necessary concessions are most likely to be wrung out of them by fear of such a body [of Socialists] than they are to be wheedled and coaxed out of them by the continual life of compromise which 'Parliamentary Socialists' would be compelled to live.

The executive of the recently formed (1883) Fabian Society, including the Webbs and George Bernard Shaw, disagreed. Committed to a policy of gradualism, the inevitability of which they took for granted, they wanted no part of Morris' militant crusade: 'Now we have no hesitation in saying that if the once hard-headed English workman came to believe that the [insurrectionary] ideas of Mr Morris were in any degree representative, the present and by no means unbrilliant prospects of Socialism in England would vanish like a dream.'

The issue was eventually joined at a meeting at London's Anderton Hotel in September, 1886. The Fabian executive tabled the substantive motion: 'That it is advisable that Socialists should organize themselves into a political party', to which Morris added the rider: 'that whereas no Parliamentary Party can exist without compromise and concession ... [thus] it would be a false step for Socialists to take part in the Parliamentary contest.' The substantive motion was carried, to widen the breach between militant and moderate wings of the embryonic movement.

Half a century had passed since the issue of extra-Parliamentary action had divided the Chartists against themselves. In the half century that lay ahead, the issue was to rent the movement time and again, to generate bitter, internecine hostilities between the factions involved. Fundamental as the differences were, however, they did nothing to dampen the euphoria that marked the foundation of the Labour Representation Committee (forerunner of the Labour Party) in February 1900. A disparate assembly, representing 65 trade unions, and three socialist societies, each committed to its own vision of the future, and how it could be achieved, it was Keir Hardie, the first Labour member to sit in the Commons, who finally cobbled together a formula on which all could agree:

> That this Conference is in favour of establishing a distinct Labour Group in Parliament who shall have their own Whips and agree on their policy, which must embrace a readiness to co-operate with any other party, for the time being, which may be engaged in promoting legislation in the direct interest of labour ... .

A correspondent for the *Clarion* described the event as 'a little cloud no bigger than a man's hand which may grow into a United Labour Party'. Percipient as he was, he was only half correct. It might well be a party, but united? And if Hardie's compromise had disguised the differences that divided the delegates, then his reference to cooperating with other parties was to aggravate the already fragile alliance. With only a handful of Members in the Commons, *realpolitic* demanded that they did whatever was necessary to promote legislation 'in the direct interest of labour', which provided the grounds for Ramsay MacDonald, Secretary of the Independent Labour Party, secretly to sign an electoral pact with the Liberals in 1903. It was within this Liberal orthodoxy that the party grew, though by 1907 Hardie himself was beginning to have doubts about the concordat: 'By another session those of us in the party who are Socialists and believe in fighting will have to get together on our own account and if we can not drag the party with us we will "gan oor ain gait".'

The very idea mocked MacDonald's quietism. Inexorably, his close association with the Liberals had mellowed his socialism to the point it was virtually indistinguishable from many of the more radical Liberal MPs, a relationship reinforced by the Asquith government's social reform programme. In his 1909 Budget, the Chancellor of the Exchequer, Lloyd George, had issued a forthright challenge to the Opposition: 'This a War Budget. It is to raise money to wage implacable war against poverty and squalidness.' While Lloyd George's challenge determined the Tories' response, it compounded Labour's dilemma. There could be no question of opposing the package, yet doing so would reinforce the impression that the party was little more than a left-wing appendage of a progressive alliance. And as the Tories' hostility intensified, so the Liberal response became radicalized. Lloyd George savaged the cant of their principles:

> I was telling you, I went down a mine the other day ... In the very next colliery to the one I descended, just a few years ago, three hundred people lost their lives. And yet when the Prime Minister and I knock on the door of these great landlords and say to them 'Here you know that these poor fellows at the risk of their lives ... Won't you give us something to keep them out of the workhouse?' They scowl at us, and we say 'Only a ha'penny, just a copper.' They say: 'You thieves!' and they turn their dogs on us, and you can hear their bark every morning.

This was the language of the militant rather than the moderate left, language which prompted the King to claim that 'it set class against class', and provoked Sir Edward Carson to complain to *The*

Times that Lloyd George has 'taken off the mask and openly preached a war of the classes'. To the Labour group in the Commons such talk was taboo; and while MacDonald was quick to endorse the Budget ('an epoch making measure'), he was equally quick to assure the House that that was because 'no Socialism was in it'.

MacDonald's protestation did little to satisfy the more radical elements of the labour movement, not least a handful of dissident Labour MPs, and a growing number of trade unionists. In 1910, unemployment was at its highest level since 1886, and still rising, while the purchasing power of the pound had fallen by a quarter since 1895, and was still falling. It was a fissile combination, of which Ben Tillett, founder of the Dockers' Union, and leader of the great dock strike of 1889, was to write: 'Britain is in an increasingly restless mood, but our movement lacks direction.' So much was easily said, the question being: What of an alternative? Tillett's long-time friend, Tom Mann, was to provide it. A former member of the Royal Commission on Labour (1894), who had preceded Mac-Donald as secretary of the Independent Labour Party, Mann quit England in 1901 to work as a political activist, first in New Zealand and then in Australia. It was there that he formulated his political credo, grounded in the belief that: 'The present system of sectional trade unionism is incapable of combating effectively the capitalist system under which the world is now suffering.'

The challenge, again, was to develop a credible alternative. Little more than a decade after Morris had campaigned for extra-Parliamentary action, without the agency to achieve his goal, syndicalism was to provide both the theory and a practice for taking politics out-of-doors. In the US the academic Daniel Da Leon, disdaining Parliamentary action, advocated that trade unions should declare war on capital, a credo that laid the foundation of International Workers of the World (IWW), while in France George Sorel had reached much the same conclusion, for his seminal work *Reflexions sur la violence* to become the handbook of the Confederation General du Travail.

Tom Mann was to become their political journeyman. In the first issue of *The Industrial Syndicalist,* published in 1910, he wrote: 'They

[Labour MPs] are revolutionary neither in their attitude towards existing society nor in respect of present day institutions ... .The engines of war to fight the workers' battle to overthrow the Capitalist class must be of the workers' own making.' Its agency? A general federation of trade unions. Its means? The strike weapon. Its object? 'To change the system of society from capitalist to socialist.'

Mann's perspective laid the groundwork for much that was to follow, the so-called Great Unrest. By the close of 1910, and encouraged by the Amalgamation Committees established by the syndicalists, the motley of dockers' and transport workers' unions combined to form the Transport Workers Federation. Within the year, the Federation's success revealed what could be achieved by collaboration. Early in 1911 strikes by Lancashire weavers and the Society of London compositors had been picked off, piecemeal, by management; but in June a localized stoppage by dockers in support of striking seamen quickly flared into national strike. By August, 100,000 workers were out in London, while in Liverpool, where two gunboats were stationed in the Mersey with their guns trained on the city, local railmen came out in sympathy with the dockers, to trigger an extension of the strike. Within the week 200,000 railmen were on strike, prompting the Home Secretary, Winston Churchill, to declare that Britain was under the control of military authorities 'practically every regiment ... having now been mobilized'. A full-scale confrontation was only avoided when the government's nerve broke and it intervened to persuade the port authorities to meet the unions and settle their demands.

Syndicalism appeared to have been vindicated, direct action having succeeded where gradualism had failed. It was an issue which, in a reprise of much that had gone before, was to expose the congenital rift in the Labour Party. While MacDonald asserted that working men had been 'goaded into revolt by agitators', and his confidant, Philip Snowden, maintained that concerted extra-Parliamentary action had no place in the Labour programme, Hardie declared: 'It is the experience gained by the strike which ultimately filters into the consciousness of the working class and makes political action a triumphant reality.' And as the internecine wrangle continued, the contest out-of-doors intensified. In 1912 more than 38 million man days were lost due to strikes, prompting the government's industrial troubleshooter, George Askwith, to reflect: 'Within comparatively short space of time there may be movements coming to a head in this country of which recent events have been a small foreshadowing.'

There is a dark irony in the fact that in 1914 the tide of industrial militancy was still running. Effectively, the outbreak of the First World War gave the lie to Askwith's fears. By the mid-summer, more than 900 stoppages had been recorded, and in July the Scottish pit owners announced that they could no longer afford to pay the seven shillings a day minimum wage and, thus, were cutting it by a shilling. The miners would have nothing of it. Only four months had passed since they had entered into a Triple Alliance with the transport workers' and railwaymen's unions, a formidable combination which, if mobilized, would have brought Britain to a standstill. A three-word telegram despatched from the War Office at 12.20am on 5 August was to avert the crisis: 'War. Germany. Act'. Six years were to pass before Ernest Bevin was to write a postscript to The Great Unrest: 'It was a period which, if the war had not broken out, would, I believe, have seen one of the greatest industrial revolts the world has ever seen.'

Four years of war marked an uneasy truce between the conflicting wings of the labour movement, which was to end with the peace if, at first, it appeared that the Party leadership had learned something from past confrontations. In its first attempt at formulating a coherent, systematic programme, *Labour and the New Social Order*, published in 1918, it rejected any further attempts to reconstitute private capitalism:

> The individualistic system of capitalist production ... with the monstrous inequalities of circumstances which it produces may, we hope, have received a death-blow. ... We, of the Labour Party, whether in opposition or in due time called upon to form an Administration, will certainly not lend a hand in its revival. On the contrary, we shall do our utmost to see that it is buried with the millions whom it has done to death.

So much for the undertaking. The reality was somewhat different. Philip Snowden had once declared that: 'the transition to Socialism will be brought about with as little hardship to existing interests as can be avoided.' The 1918 programme echoed his sentiments. Drafted by, amongst others, Sidney Webb, if not the author, then a leading exponent of the inevitability of gradualism, *The New Social Order* stressed the role that Parliamentary legislation would play in the transformation of capitalism. Meanwhile, Direct Action remained taboo. The problem was that, deprived of effective representation in the Commons, there was little that the Party leadership could do to check the wholesale dismantling of the war economy involving, as it had done, the control of key industries, the regulation of the import, distribution and price of food, and, critically, of a 1915 agreement by the unions to abandon strike action for the duration of the war.

By the war's end, it seemed that *laissez-faire* was obsolescent if not obsolete. The illusion was shortlived. Although four years of war had seriously undermined the UK economy, it appeared that capitalism had lost none of its former rapacity, and unions grew restless again. In 1919 wholesale prices rose by 72 per cent, against a 20 per cent increase in the average wage, while everywhere queues at the Labour Exchanges lengthened, unemployment rising by 12.2 per cent. It was all very well for Lloyd George to talk of building a land fit for heroes, but a growing body of trade unionists had had more than enough of his sophistry. Throughout the spring and summer industry was racked by a series of strikes, to be followed in the autumn by a walk out of railmen which Lloyd George denounced as part of an 'anarchist conspiracy'. The charge was unfounded, the reality being that if labour felt cheated of its proper influence in the political system, then it was up to the unions to redress the balance, prompting the miners' leader Frank Hodges to reflect:

> I am astonished that, in view of the impotence of the Labour Party, caused by circumstances over which it has no control, it does not more frequently come to the industrial movement and say 'We are overweighted and crushed by a great political despotism. Come to our

> assistance in order that we may have power at our elbow to shatter the institution and remould one on better lines.'

The challenge was explicit, the response muted. In 1918, Sidney Webb dismissed the notion of such a power-shift as a 'shibboleth', to be labelled a defeatist by Mann. Seemingly the situation was irreconcilable, as much about the ends to be achieved as the means to achieve them. And as the economic conditions continued to deteriorate during the early 1920s, so the conflict for the hearts and minds of socialism intensified, with the miners playing an increasingly militant role. In 1919, the Sankey Commission called for the nationalization of the industry by 1922, and for 'the reorganisation and control of the industry centrally'. The miners were delighted, the pit owners incensed, and Lloyd George in a quandary. Either he subscribed to the majority report of the Commission, or settled for that of the sole dissenter, Sir Arthur Duckham. He opted for the latter, and on August 18, 1919, rose at the Despatch Box to announce his decision: 'The Government have come to the conclusion that the state should not purchase the business of mines, and certainly not run them.'

The scene was set for a bruising conflict that was to expose the extent of the schism in the labour movement. For four years successive administrations wrangled in an attempt to resolve the coal question, and in January 1924, Labour formed its first government with Liberal support. An unstable combination, its life was short lived, MacDonald leading a push-me-pull-you administration in the style of the Duke of Plaza Toro, for when the left cried 'Forward', the Liberals cried 'Back', and when the Liberals cried 'Back' the left cried 'Traitors'. Even before MacDonald had formed his government, the radical Tom Johnson had warned that: 'If the Labour Party were to betray the working class by allying itself with a Capitalist party, the Labour Party is finished' – a lethal charge in the party's lexicon. His forebodings were quickly realized. Twice during its short life the government announced that it was prepared to use the Emergency Powers Act, first against striking dockers, then against railmen. It was a betrayal too far as far as the unions were concerned. On 8 October the government fell, damned by the left from the day it took office, and twice damned when it fell for having failed socialism.

For the left, once again, the lesson was clear, there could be no compromising with capitalism. As for the party leadership there appeared to be no other alternative. Convinced that Labour's future could only be secured by reinforcing its gradualist credentials, the leadership progressively whittled down the scope of its programme, more especially as far as public ownership was concerned. *Labour and the New Social Order* had pledged to workers 'the full fruits of their industry ... upon the basis of the common ownership of the means of production'. Following the débâcle of 1924, the undertaking was rewritten in altogether more ambiguous terms, promising only that public ownership would be restricted 'to the larger and more widely used public services'. And if the Labour leadership was quick to retreat from its pledges, the Tories were as quick to exploit the party's disarray, and launch a major offensive against labour. Their prime target? The miners.

Faced with falling demand, the coal owners reverted to their timeworn practice of demanding a cut in miners' wages and an extension of their working hours. In July 1925, the Prime Minister, Stanley Baldwin, extended the offensive, warning all workers that they, too, would have to accept wage cuts. The response was immediate. The rail and transport workers' unions – the Triple Alliance reactivated – pledged themselves to support the miners' call for a complete stoppage of all movements of coal to be reinforced, if necessary, by a sympathetic strike. Baldwin temporized, and on the offer of peace terms the strike was called off. The respite was only temporary, however, Baldwin recognizing that his rhetoric was not matched by the government's capacity to contain a major industrial dispute. And having called for what amounted to a nine-month cooling-off period, during which the coal owners would be paid a temporary subsidy, primarily to meet miners' wages, and the Samuel Commission was established to report on the case, the government set about making plans for a major confrontation which it certainly anticipated, if not engineered.

As for Labour's Parliamentary leadership, the threat of a general strike was regarded if not with hostility, then with embarrassment, in part because it would render them redundant, in part because it would jeopardize their gradualist strategy. The result, as the Labour historian G. D. H. Cole later concluded, was 'a mixture of inopportune pacifism and over confidence', compounded in Ramsay Mac-Donald's case by an outright rejection of direct action. The charge may have done something to account for MacDonald's appointment of his aide, Jimmy Thomas, to the TUC's Special Industrial Committee responsible for co-ordinating union action: 'to defend any principle of an industrial character which might be deemed vital by allied organisations'. As both an MP and General Secretary of the National Union of Railwaymen, Thomas had little time for militancy, going so far as to deny, explicitly, that he was a socialist when asked the question during a libel action he had brought in 1921.

While the government accelerated its preparations for the show-down that was to come, and its powerfully disciplined Organisation for the Maintenance of Supplies counted down the days to the one-word telegram, 'Action', the TUC Special Industrial Committee equivocated, spending the first three months of the truce deciding whether or not it should meet. Even after the Samuel Commission published its report in March, 1926, which concluded that there could be no alternative to a temporary wage cut, the Committee continued to play its dilatory games, so that with only 72 hours remaining until the subsidy ended, no organization to conduct a strike had been countenanced, let alone put in place.

On Friday 30 April, the subsidy ended, and that evening lockout notices were posted on collieries throughout Britain. Twenty-four hours later, on May Day, 1926, the General Council of the TUC asked for a mandate to call a General Strike. When the final figures were announced – For: 3,653,529; Against: 49,111 – Ramsay Mac-Donald and Jimmy Thomas joined in singing the Red Flag. The General Strike lasted nine days, but it was lost before it began. The feminist MP Susan Lawrence might enthuse: 'We are living in momentous times, on the eve of great things.' Beatrice Webb disagreed. 'There will not even be a revolutionary reaction. Thomas and Baldwin will see to that.' She was right.

Five days into the stoppage, Thomas was already colluding in the lie that support for the miners among railwaymen was collapsing (in fact, only two per cent of the workforce of the four rail unions had returned to work by 8 May), but the rumour sapped at the already flagging confidence of TUC's General Council, and by 10 May there was growing support for a hastily revised but little improved version of the Samuel Commission's original report. Twenty-four hours later the miners' leaders, Arthur Cook and Herbert Smith, were presented with what amounted to a *fait accompli* by the General Council, and on being asked whether the government would deliver on Samuel's promise, Thomas replied: 'You may not trust my word, but won't you trust the word of a British gentleman who has been governor of Palestine?' Whether or not they did, it made no difference. The Council's mind was already made up, Thomas having dismissed any doubts that remained, asserting that the miners were 'not trade unionists in the proper sense'. The following day the strike was called off. The government had demanded unconditional surrender, which was exactly what they had achieved.

It was not only the strike that the government succeeded in breaking in May 1926, but also the political will of the trade union leadership, and with it, the will of much of the labour movement. Seemingly, the bogey of syndicalism had finally been laid, for even if the rank and file of the movement had been capable of mounting a concerted attack on capital, their leaders had neither the taste nor the temperament to engage in such a contest. MacDonald couldn't but agree: 'The General Strike is a weapon that cannot be wielded for industrial purposes. It is clumsy and ineffectual. It has no goal which, when reached, can be regarded as victory ... I hope that the result will be a thorough reconsideration of trade union tactics.'

Buoyed by his own rhetoric, of which Beatrice Webb was to write: 'Where he has lacked integrity is in *posing* as a Socialist and occasionally using revolutionary jargon', MacDonald's innate conservatism become more marked between Labour's first and second administrations. Increasingly impatient with what he regarded as 'the mood and manners' of the militant wing of the party, he came to believe that there was, in fact, little to distinguish between the policies of his own and his Tory opponents, to reflect that eventually 'the partition between us and them will be so thin that they might as well break it down and come over to the Socialist camp'. The future cast long shadows. Meanwhile, MacDonald and party leadership underestimated the bitterness engendered by what was regarded as a betrayal of the miners, notably by Jimmy Maxton, leader of the ILP, and the mining communities themselves. Not that the ILP challenge to gradualism was the sole product of 'frustrated anarchism' as its critics liked to believe. Following the fall of the first Labour government, the Party-within-a-Party published *Socialism in our Time* (1927), which it offered as a radical alternative to the obscurantist policies of the Labour leadership, and challenged 'the deadening idea that socialism can only be established by slow gradualism over generations of time'. Morris had declared that time was the bondsman of capitalism. Now it was time that it served other masters.

Whilst the ILP continued to adopt a hard line, the General Council of the TUC settled for an altogether more ameliorative approach. The war economy had revealed what could be achieved by adopting a measure of collaboration between management and labour, and it was this corporatist vision that laid the foundations for the General Council's commitment to creating: 'a new industrial order ... not by way of a social explosion, but by a planned reconstruction in which unions will assume a larger share of control in directing industrial changes.' In its five-point programme of 1928, *Labour and the Nation*, the party leadership subscribed to much the same goal: 'to convert industry step by step ... from a contest for private gain into a co-operative undertaking carried on for the service of the community and amenable to its control.' Maxton was derisive. Nothing could be more deceptive than the right's apparent commitment to socialism: 'A Labour government cannot run capitalism any more than Baldwin or the others.'

All too soon, events were to prove him right. The world economy was already in poor shape when Labour returned to power in May 1929. Whereas world trade had grown by 25 per cent and more in every decade between 1830 and 1914, it grew by only 8 per cent during the 1920s, with punishing consequences for the UK economy heavily dependent, as it was, on its exporting capacity. In the three decades to 1914, UK exports rose by an average of 3 per cent a year. In the post-war years, exports fell to a fifth below that figure, with all that that implied in employment terms. Although subject to variations, the underlying trend for unemployment rose consistently from the mid-1920s onwards, to become the issue that dominated the 1929 election, as the Liberals were to dominate the unemployment debate.

Lloyd George may have been 'this goat footed bard, this half human visitor from the … enchanted woods of Celtic antiquity' of Keynes's description, but he was one of the first to appreciate the revolutionary significance of Keynes's economic theories, most notably that during downswings in the economic cycle governments should intervene actively to stimulate demand and curb unemployment. In the sixpenny pamphlet *We Can Conquer Unemployment*, which appeared under Lloyd George's name, the stated aim was unequivocal:

> At the moment, individual enterprise alone cannot restore the situation (unemployment) within a time for which we can wait. The state must therefore lend its aid and, by a deliberate policy of national development, help to set going at full speed the great machinery of industry.

The Tories were contemptuous, the Labour leadership dismissive. Following the fall of the first Labour government, Churchill had written: 'The Treasury mind and the Snowden mind embraced each other with the fervour of two long-separated kindred lizards.' The barb was to prove well founded. Committed to Treasury orthodoxy involving, as it did, a deflationary policy in pursuit of a balanced budget, Snowden had no time for Keynes's nostrums.

As the situation deteriorated, so Snowden's position hardened. Described by J. K. Galbraith as 'the slaughter of the innocents', the Wall Street crash of October 1929 precipitated a crisis that was to rack the world, and with it, the UK economy. When the Labour government took office, 9.5 per cent of the workforce, or 1,163,000 men and women, were registered as unemployed. A year later, the figure numbered 1,912,000, or 15.4 per cent of the workforce, and by Christmas 1930 a fifth of the working population, totalling 2,725,000 men and women, was out of work. This was 'the economic blizzard' (Ramsay MacDonald) which, in 1931, would blow the Labour administration away. In his February Budget, Snowden's message was straightforward: to balance the books, public sector spending would have to be curbed which, in practice, meant slashing benefit payments to the unemployed.

Even Snowden could not have imagined where his policy would lead. On the last day of July 1931, the May Committee, appointed to examine plans for reducing public expenditure, forecast a £120 million budget deficit, to be balanced by a 20 per cent cut in the standard rate of benefit, and a £37 million reduction in a range of other, government funded programmes. Ironically, though the report reflected the City's mind-set, it reinforced the capital markets concerns about the vulnerable state of the UK economy. Arguably, in fact, the crisis that was yet to come was, in part, of the City's own making, for in making a bogey of public expenditure it was eventually to fall victim to its own, inflated, fears.

In microcosm, the first three weeks of August, 1931, reflected the seemingly timeless clash between capital and labour. While Keynes argued that Britain should devalue by 25 per cent as the first step to 'organising prosperity', the City, with the Snowden and the Treasury's backing, insisted that there was no alternative to making swingeing cuts in public expenditure, culminating in a demand too far – a punitive cut in Unemployment Benefits and the introduction of a means test for all applicants.

The end, when it came, came quickly. On Saturday 22 August, members of the Cabinet split on whether to make any further concessions to the City, and authorized MacDonald to inform the King that they had placed their resignation in his hands. George V, however, asked MacDonald to reconsider his decision, and, whilst the opposition watched and waited in the anteroom of power, the bankers remained intractable. Either the government met their conditions, or they would renege on a promised loan.

The following day, Sunday 23 August, the Cabinet accepted the bankers' ultimatum, but only on a split vote, coupled with a threat of mass resignation by the dissenters. For a second time in 24 hours, MacDonald returned to the Palace to tender his government's resignation. This time it was accepted, with the proviso that Mac-Donald consider forming a National Government with the support of both Conservatives and Liberals. At 11.55 on Monday, 24 August, a brief statement was issued by the Press Association: 'His Majesty the King invited the Prime Minister, Mr Stanley Baldwin, and Sir Herbert Samuel to Buckingham Palace this morning, and the formation of a national government is under consideration.'

Yet again, it appeared that there could be no compromising with capitalism. Indeed, as one Labour MP was later to reflect, in pursuing a policy of gradualism the Party came close to compromising itself out of existence. He knew what he was about. In the election of October 1931, Labour lost 256 seats, to return 52 Members to the Commons, the lowest figure since before the war.

The débâcle of 1931 was to traumatize the Labour Party. Only three years had passed since being returned to office with a working majority, yet now? Now, once again, the talk was of MacDonald's apostasy, and the apparent delight that Snowden took in disavowing his socialist roots: 'Every day from the first day of the election campaign to the eve of the poll I launched attacks on my late Labour colleagues.' It was all very well for Arthur Henderson, the former Foreign Secretary, to assert that 'nothing had happened either to the Party or to its electoral position to warrant any scrapping of our programme', but even for moderates such as Jimmy Clynes, Mac-Donald's Home Secretary, the disillusionment was too deep rooted, too corrosive for that: 'Socialism had not failed. We had never yet begun to try even a little part of it.'

Keir Hardie accepted that the Party would always be a marriage of ideological convenience. In the 1930s, the full, divisive nature of the marriage was to be exposed. In 1932, the ILP cut its links with the Party that it had helped to found, for it to be replaced by the Socialist League as the forcing ground of socialism. Named in honour of William Morris, Stafford Cripps, a founder of the renascent League, had caught something of Morris's commitment to 'making Socialist' in his maiden speech in the Commons. A nephew of Beatrice Webb, Cripps had little but contempt for his aunt's brand of socialism: 'We are not here to do hospital work for the Juggernaut of Capitalism. We are here to stop that Juggernaut from his progress through the world ... The one thing that *is not inevitable now is gradualness.*'

If the breach was seemingly irreparable, then it was to be compounded at the Party Conference of 1932. Although still bruised by memories of MacDonald's apostasy, the Party's National Executive Committee, fearful of their own activists, continued to play the moderate role, to table a series of resolutions that were as bereft of real substance, as they were ambiguous in content, maintaining that it was 'not possible to specify exactly in advance the order in which a majority Labour government would proceed with its measures of economic reorganisation'.

The left wanted nothing of such blandness. They had lived for too long, had had altogether too much of appeasing 'the Juggernaut' of capitalism. In its place, they passed a resolution asserting 'that the main object of the Labour Party is the establishment of socialism', and reiterated the resolution of 1918: 'that the common ownership of the means of production and distribution is the only means by which producers by hand and brain will be able to secure the full fruits of their industry.' In his memoirs, Hugh Dalton was to write of a dream he had at the time: 'a dream in which he saw himself at a Labour Party conference moving a resolution to nationalize the Solar System. This was at first regarded as a brilliant idea, but towards the close of the debate a Socialist Leaguer got up at the back of the hall and moved an amendment to add the words "and the Milky Way".'

A rogue member of the establishment, Dalton (Eton and Cambridge) had no time for the 'impossibilists' radical agenda, more especially the attack mounted by Cripps and Harold Laski, Professor of Political Science at the London School of Economics, on what they had come to regard as the magic circle of power – legislature, crown, and capital – that colluded to promote the illusion of a liberal democracy in order to perpetuate its own hegemony. Nothing was explicit, all was implied, a gentlemen's agreement to secure what R. H. Tawney called 'our religion of inequality' in the interests of the establishment. Laski, anathematized by Dalton as the 'Devil in the Labour Party', agreed. Convinced that George V had played a significant role in the downfall of the second Labour government, he was later to write: 'The new Cabinet was born of a Palace revolution ... The Crown has rarely exerted so profound an influence in modern times.'

While Laski and Cripps contested the constitutional high ground, to fortify the Ernest Bevin's conviction that 'intellectuals of the left were the people that stabbed you in the back', an altogether more practical issue was racking the Party. Labour's commitment to a programme of nationalization was all very well so far as it went, but the question remained: How far should it go? Given office, how would the newly nationalized industries be managed? By whom would they be run? In short, was the democratic management of industry reality or myth? Pragmatists such as Herbert Morrison, leader of the London County Council, were clear as to the answer – to be too democratic at the outset would jeopardize the entire project, the need being to recruit 'the best available directive ability and technical skill', in other words, the existing 'captains of industry'. As for worker control it had no place in their programme, worker participation in management being limited to questions about working conditions.

Realistic or otherwise, it formed no part of the left's agenda. The covenant of 1918 had been clear as to where the future control of nationalized industries should be located, whereas Morrison's proposals would simply replace capitalist by bureaucratic management, damning workers to remain 'the hewers of wood and drawers of water' that they had always been. In 1933, the Party Conference rejected Morrison's formula in its entirety, committing the Party to the view that the workers' 'right to an effective share in the control and direction of socialized industries should be acknowledged by law'. For Clem Attlee, elected leader of the party in 1935, the debates of the early 1930s established the fact that workers' control was 'an essential part of the new order' providing, as it did, a bolder conception of the economic role of any future Labour government, in which capitalism was not so much reconstructed as superseded.

The lessons of the MacDonald era had been hard learned. The Labour leadership of the late 1930s was pledged not to repeat them. Given power, there would be no going back on introducing a measure of worker control in the future management of nationalized industries. Even Dalton, elitist that he was, accepted that any future Labour government 'must start off with a well planned rush' involving, amongst other things, the nationalization of the shipbuilding and heavy chemical industries. And in a mirror image of the events of 1926, Attlee made it clear that an incoming Labour administration would 'unhesitatingly seek emergency powers' if it met any resistance to its programme. The post-war years were to test not only the leadership's resolve in carrying out its programme, but equally to resolving the problem of precisely what the democratic control of industry might mean, and how it might be realized.

Chapter 6

Labour and the New Social Order

Paddy Maguire

At the Labour Party Conference in 1949, held just four years after the apparently epochal landslide victory of 1945, one delegate, himself an MP, and not one noted for factional party politicking, warned his listeners that,

> ... a detached observer who did not know the movement would have drawn the conclusion that the two ways we had to proceed were either State Socialism or, alternatively, private enterprise ... There is a distinct danger that when we pass out of the next period, which is not too dissimilar to the N.E.P. period of the Russian Revolution, we shall then go forward again with the establishment of more power in the hands of the centre. Power corrupts. Too much power in one set of hands can take us along the very road that we are trying to avoid. Democracy and economic democracy means a diversion of power and not its complete centralisation.

The speaker, Percy Daines, MP for East Ham North, did indeed have a particular axe to grind. As a lifelong cooperator, he was pushing the virtues of cooperation as a 'third way', but in doing so he was also echoing the concerns about the nationalized industries, the bureaucratization of production, the distinct absence of industrial democracy and the developing tendency of many party officials, and even more of most Ministers, to denounce any opposition to policy, and in particular any direct action, as disloyal at best and positively subversive at worst. Already, the schisms, not the internal party sectarianism (which could often be simple camouflage for personal ambition and political placing, and could be easily caricatured as 'left' and 'right'), but the real schisms were coming to the fore. These were about the nature and use of power; they were about the extent (or limitation) of representative democracy, and about the socialization, as opposed to the nationalization, of industry. They were about the primacy of electoral engineering through managing consumption, about the rights (and wrongs) of trades union power in an expansive economy predicated on full, or, to some early critics, over-full employment. They were about the role of Britain in a rapidly changing world.

Such schisms would dominate Party affairs and Party politics whether in power or in opposition over the coming decades. The role of the Party might change somewhat when in power, the tone of the discourse might be moderated through considerations of electoral calculus or the theatre of Party conferences and the tortured prose of the official Party policy-making apparatus, but they would come to the fore again and again at moments of crisis and conflict. Much of the argument was, of course, about what the Party represented – or ought to represent. Here two considerations were crucial. The first was the structure (ideologically as well as formally) of the Party. It was constituted after the reconstruction of 1918 as an uneven balance between three constituencies. Firstly, professional politicians, many of whose upper ranks had deserted the Liberal Party once it had entered terminal decline after 1922. Secondly, the constituency parties which provided the electoral foot soldiers for the metropolitan general staff, and whose role also grew with the massive extension of local government's 'welfare' agenda (health, housing and education in particular) in the inter-war period. Thirdly, the trades unions whose financial support and, even more importantly, massive voting power dominated the party arena in general and conference votes in particular. While this may have been the constitutional architecture of the Party, the reality at local level was often somewhat different. The Party rank and file, particularly the male rank and file, were often trades union activists as well as Party activists (though other trades union activists owed allegiance to other parties). They were also, as were many female party activists, adherents of the other – and, in membership terms, the largest constituent part of the socialist commonwealth – the Co-operative Movement (whose political arm, since its inception during the closing stages of the First World War had been an appendage of the Labour Party).

The second major determinant of Labour's ideological and organizational schizophrenia was its history. This was a Party deeply bruised by the experience of the thirties, both the 'betrayal' of 1931, and by the internecine conflicts within and between 'left' factions loosely clustered around the Third International's 'Class Against Class' and 'Popular Front' periods. It was in the thirties that the internal disciplinary machinery, to be used so remorselessly in the fifties, was first fully honed with such luminaries as Cripps, Bevin and Strauss, all expelled along with a clutch of Party activists. As in the 1950s, and indeed in the later 1980s, conflict was as much about electoral calculation as about ideological purity. This was a Party dedicated, in its higher echelons at least, to power – that is, to Parliamentary power. The brief flirtation with (minority) power in the 1920s had clearly whetted the collective appetite – it was as much fear that Cripps's extra-Parliamentary, Popular Front-based Petition Campaign would detract from Labour's electoral prospects as it was differing political perspectives which dictated the Southport expulsions. It was also the case, as would become the norm on such occasions, that the process was heavily laced with the personal antipathy of a number of Labour's would-be power brokers (in particular Dalton, and the perennial aspiring, but equally perennially uncrowned, leader Morrison). In this context, Labour's will to power should not be underestimated. It was, among other things, an electoral machine, perhaps most noticeably in the dominant local labour fiefdoms which were beginning to emerge in the 1950s, and would gradually be cemented in place, particularly in the industrial heartlands of the North. They would flower, if that is the correct term for such ruthlessly single party fiefdoms as T. Dan Smith's Newcastle, in the 1950s.

It was, though, an almost nineteenth-century version of political power that enthralled Labour leaders, perhaps itself a reflection of the long-drawn-out suffrage campaigns from the 1820s to (for female voters) the 1920s. Labour's perspective, as Daines instinctively recognized, was (and is) unreservedly statist – whether of the national or the local state. Capturing Parliamentary power, controlling the legislative levers of power, was (and is) its *raison d'être*. At times the commitment to the achievement and maintenance of power, of being in government rather than in politics, could be overwhelming, and would override all other loyalties or considerations – indeed even override other aspects and outcrops of state power. As Hugh Gaitskell noted in his diary in 1950, teetering on the edge of electoral disaster, and faced with industrial militancy in the electricity generating stations,

> I saw a great deal of Citrine during the strike and was much impressed by his determination and fairness. As things developed it became clear that there was a fundamental difference of view between the B[ritish] E[electricity] A[authority] and ourselves on the one hand and the Ministry of Labour on the other. The latter were concerned with ending the strike: whereas we were concerned with smashing the strikers.

Such was his concern about the impact of union power that Gaitskell wanted simply to outlaw strikes in the industry. Gaitskell's ally in such determined anti-union campaigning was no fellow public school-educated intellectual (as Gaitskell's party opponents could caricature him) but a veteran of the Labour movement. Walter Citrine was an electrician by trade. He had become a trade's union official (in the ETU, the union which was causing Gaitskell such concern) by the age of 27, and had cut his teeth as TUC General Secretary during the General Strike. He had served as TUC General Secretary for 20 years before moving effortlessly to successive positions in the newly nationalized sector, first with the National Coal Board, and then as Chairman of the BEA from 1947 to 1957.

Nor was it a simple left/right internal party alignment. Nye Bevan, darling of the left, was pressing the BEA to take civil action against the strikers for breach of contract, and Herbert Morrison would soon be pressing for mandatory ballots, compulsory arbitration and other measures to curb strikes in what were deemed to be essential industries. Indeed, a clutch of ministers were involved in secret discussions with the TUC in an abortive attempt to win support for the Attorney General's proposals to introduce new legal restraints on strikes (which to some extent prefigured Barbara Castle's *In Place Of Strife,* and subsequent legal enactments in the 1970s and 1980s). Indeed, Castle's *Diaries* would record her own secret meetings with George Woodcock (TUC General Secretary), Aubrey Jones (Chairman Prices and Incomes Board) and John Davies (General Secretary Confederation of British Industries) in 1968, where 'they speak frankly and in remarkable harmony about things they will be quarrelling about publicly', as she sought to introduce new industrial legislation.

Much of the problem, to contemporaries, was the massive extension of state power occasioned both by the necessities of war, and by Labour's commitment to 'the new social order'. Although such problems were exacerbated by the post-war economic crisis (and successive Labour administrations in the sixties and seventies would find themselves attempting to operate in similar periods of economic collapse and crisis), part of the problem lay in the architecture of the post-war settlement, and in the nature of the British Parliamentary structure. Successive governments were never sure whether the great new nationalized industries, created as singular corporations, were essentially departments of state, or new forms of economic organization meant to deliver not just improved efficiency out of the shambles of, frequently small-scale, competitive companies that dominated much of British economic output, but also some version of industrial democracy. In a very short space of time the latter would become not just an abstract ideological debate, or an apparent Party touchstone through the seemingly endless battles over Clause Four, but a structural impediment to the realization of that very 'new social order' which had been so trumpeted in 1945. This was certainly the case for some of the Party's leaders, but it was even more the case for some of its activists.

From some perspectives, again in rhetorical terms that would become even more entrenched in the 1960s and 1970s (and be virtually institutionalized as a New Labour ideological bedrock), it could seem, quite simply, that the workers were not up to it. They had let the Party down (or the State, or the newly nationalized industry) by pursuing their own – as opposed to the 'national', or Party, or economic – interest. As Bevan told the Party Conference,

> (t)hese great industries are now in our possession. We are responsible for them. We are entitled to look to the workers in these industries not merely for demands that we should attend to their rights but to expect from them a sense of public responsibility and service in the Industries ... [then] they will have proved that they can be entrusted with safeguarding the nation's interests.

Herbert Morrison would put it more succinctly where, during the transition to the new social order 'the first economic duty of each man and woman is to the nation as a whole'. 'We' and 'they', or 'us' and 'them' was precisely what the socialization of industry was supposed to replace. From almost the outset of the 1945 government it had been apparent to some that there was a danger inherent in the model of centralized economic power, predicated upon centralized political power, not merely not extending but actively undermining the rhetoric of industrial democracy. As early as 1946, Morrison, in many ways the most populist politician in the Government, was warning that they 'should not slip into a position in which the miners or railway workers were simply working for a fresh set of employers'. But it was not just from the lofty perspective of Ministerial power that the chasm appeared unbridged. To some it even appeared to be extending as the demands of large-scale industrial organization, and the demands of political accountability, appeared to result in relentless bureaucratization, and in the remorseless rise of the professional managerial class to administer the new state corporations. A member of the Dorset Federation of Labour Parties, who also boasted membership of the Railway Clerks Association, complained bitterly that nationalization had brought with it a sixfold increase in supervisory staff, and 'much extravagance in the use of special trains and motor cars'. Report after report would catalogue the growing alienation of workers in the newly nationalized industries, and the growing frustration at their burgeoning bureaucratic structure. While Attlee reached for General Slim for advice (more 'esprit de corps' was the solution, quite how it was to be achieved was somewhat absent from his resumé of his discussions), most other leading Labour politicians, like Cripps, Gaitskell, Barnes and Isaacs, dismissed the thrust for industrial democracy as at best syndicalism and at worst Communist-inspired subversion. Nor was it only in terms of internal industrial organization that the new social order rapidly became the old ideological heresy.

Increasingly, and long before Wilson's riposte to the Bennites' alleged intent on transforming Marks & Spencer (in the days when it was assumed to be a model of capitalist efficiency and market sensitivity) into a newly nationalized version of the Co-op, leading Labour politicians were retreating not just from any idea of industrial democracy, but from what were increasingly taken to be the electoral perils of government involvement in the nationalized industries. It was not only that, as a 1951 report for the Cabinet put it, there was 'little positive enthusiasm for the new order of things', not least because of a growing belief that the significant growth in what the report termed 'salaried staff' had 'caused a sense of discouragement among the ordinary workers', but also that such industries compared poorly, in terms of efficiency, with the private sector. As Wilson observed in 1950, when analysing the reasons for Labour's apparently poor performance, 'very many votes were being lost through fears of ultimate nationalisation of industries, not to mention shops which would probably never be taken over at all'. Wilson's perspective is revealing not just for the implicit rejection of an industrial strategy put in place just six years before, but also because it was so predicated on the calculus of Parliamentary democracy. Although Labour had slid into opposition, and the 1950s would witness a bitter internal party war on the origins and consequences of that electoral defeat, it had recorded its highest ever share of the vote at 48.8 per cent (against 48 per cent for the Conservatives), and had polled more votes (13,944,605) than had the new Conservative Government. Perhaps even more revealing is the fact that this total of votes was greater than the votes it garnered in the Parliamentary landslides of 1945, 1966, 1997 and 2001. Nevertheless, those intra-party battles, together with assumptions about the erosion of class-based politics in the later 1950s, would go on to dominate much of the Party's electoral strategies and public posturing in the 1960s and early 1970s. Unnecessary perhaps but arguably predictable since to professional politicians it is seats, not votes, that are the currency of power.

The response to perceived electoral failure was not only revealing, it was to have a significant affect on Labour's future trajectory. Even though the Party won a narrow overall majority in the 1950 General Election, securing 13,266,176 votes, it was treated as a failure. The National Executive Committee rapidly put together an analysis which Morrison authored as *The Recent General Election And The Next*. At the core of the response was the assumption that Labour's historic strategy was wrong. Although, in many ways, it owed its existence as a meaningful political force to the trades unions' decision to abandon the Liberal Party to pursue legislative influence through the Labour Representation Committee, some key figures now began to see such associations as electorally damaging. Winning seats did not mean winning votes per se, it meant winning marginal votes in the handful of key marginal seats which dominated British General Elections throughout the period. The massive majorities of the industrial heartlands were meaningless in this electoral calculus (other than as much sought after safe seats for aspiring career politicians); they could be taken for granted. In the wake of comparative defeat the Party's inquest focused on its representative function.

To Morrison and his supporters (and, indeed, to some recent historians), it seemed evident that Labour was seeking to represent the wrong constituency. From this viewpoint, the trades union interest, in representing producers, was costing Labour votes. In particular, Morrison was concerned that the changing structure of the economy was isolating the Party as 'a Labour government based solely on the working class would not enjoy as much authority as one based on the support of all the useful people'. Of even greater concern to Morrison was the role of female voters who, as a number of recent historians have pointed out, were largely not producers but consumers, and who bore the brunt of rationing, queuing, food shortages and the other outward manifestations of austerity in a planned economy, while their male counterparts experienced the benefits of full employment, job security and rising real wages. To Morrison it was crucial:

> ... married women are increasingly thinking for themselves politically ... it may be that even some of the working class housewives went wrong from our point of view, and it is probable that this may have happened among a substantial number of middle class housewives ... the needs of the consumer and the needs of the housewife must be recognized as a real factor in politics and Party policy and propaganda should recognize it.

Nothing concentrated the political mind so much as defeat or the fear of defeat. To Christopher Mayhew, who would be a recurrent figure in Labour Party politics until his defection to the Liberal Party in 1974, it was a simple choice: 'it was important that the Labour Party should stand as the representatives of the consumer rather than as a party of planning'. Mayhew's was a departure which presaged later party splits. He was heir to Ernest Bevin's Parliamentary seat (though, given his Haileybury and Oxford education, not to the latter's class allegiances), and was Labour's first TV 'Party Political' presenter in 1951. He lost his seat at the election.

The democracy of the market place (one pound, one vote) was to be a recurrent theme as industrial democracy, however loosely defined, was sunk without trace, and as planning, nationalization, controls and other aspects of the planned economy were deemed electorally suicidal. Two of the key elements of the 1945 new social order, 'socialization of industry' and a planned economy (however loosely defined), were to be rapidly abandoned in favour of a new, dynamic, consumer 'you ought not to never have had it so good', target-driven (housing completions, export growth, school constructions, etc.) universe. The socialist commonwealth was to be moved from new Jerusalem to New Town (presided over no doubt by a Board of dignitaries largely composed of ex senior civil servants and ex trades union officials, liberally sprinkled with Party-nominated apparatchiks of no particularly discernible political persuasion).

Consumption not production would be the electoral litmus test in this world, and 'managing the economy' (rather than 'economic management') would be the perceived test of electoral viability.

Nor was this simply a question of presentation. This was to be New Labour before anyone had thought of the term, rapidly abandoning much of the certainty of the 1940s for the uncertainties of the 1950s. By 1955, the NEC was proudly retreating to some point in the nineteenth century insisting, in its manifesto *The Individual and Society*, that 'We must set out to prove that Labour is the true inheritor of the liberal tradition'. As Douglas Jay, our man in Whitehall, and a minister in both the Attlee and Wilson administrations, put it somewhat later, in an article in 1959, after yet another electoral defeat:

> We are in danger of fighting under the label of a class which no longer exists ... What the public wants is a vigorous, radical, open-minded party. The word 'nationalisation' has become damaging to the Labour Party ... if Labour is going to win, we must remove the first two fatal handicaps: the class 'image' and the myth of 'nationalisation'. We must modernize ourselves quickly into a vigorous, radical, expansionist, open-minded Party representing – and being seen to represent – everybody who wants reform and expansion.

Jay's perceptions were clearly informed by the contemporary debates on the déclassé repercussions of affluence. He specifically refers to 'motor workers in the estates', clearly presaging perhaps the most influential sociological study of the early 1960s, Goldthorpe and Lockwood's *The Affluent Worker In The Class Structure*. This study appeared to give scientific credence to the triumph of consumption over class, though its findings were seriously invalidated by the rise of industrial militancy, particularly in the motor industry on which the study focussed, in the later 1960s and 1970s. But Jay's perceptions also reflected a deep distrust of his own constituency. In his autobiography, he recalls with obvious approval the changing class composition of his Battersea Labour Party, now informed (presumably in pre-Militant days) 'by a steady stream of young men and women who had recently come down from universities, new or old'.

His mentor, Hugh Dalton, whom he had served as personal assistant during his wartime tenure at the Board of Trade, had been even blunter in his aversions to working-class representatives, recording in his own diary on the occasion of Attlee's 70th birthday presentation the 'swarms of co-operators – all looking alike, small, stout, spectacled and insignificant ... dullards.' The personal antipathies of the respectively Winchester-, Oxford-, Eton- and Cambridge-educated ministers were more than personal – they spoke of the deep distrust of indigenous working-class organization, and of indigenous working-class organizations, which ensured that successive Labour administrations failed to conceive of democratic, representative forms existing much beyond the boundaries of Westminster.

Jay's concerns had already figured prominently in Cabinet reappraisals of strategy in the wake of the 1950 election. Jay's own solution, from his position at the Treasury, was 'competitive socialism', a sort of New Labour National Health Service mix of state and private corporations competing in the same sector. To Gaitskell it was clear that 'we should get rid of monopoly practises and let competition work'. To Wilson, who had gained considerable publicity as the incoming President of the Board of Trade with a 'bonfire of controls', it was obvious that,

> ... in future the Party should prepare its policy from the consumers point of view. We should treat electors more as consumers and less as producers. There was a need for a Consumers' Charter which would embody the setting up of Consumers' Advice Centres and the use of permanent price control. It would be easy, from the consumers point of view, to stage an attack on inefficiency and high cost in the private sector.

Citizens Advice Bureau and Shirley Williams as Secretary of State for Consumer Protection and Prices seemed a long way from the democratization of industry trumpeted in 1945, and even further away from the radical campaigns for nationalization of mines and railways in the late 1910s and early 1920s which had been so significant in the Party's early years. Indeed it might seem that even the democratically emaciated form of nationalized industry board survived more as a result of the electoral victory of the Conservatives –

mistakenly believing this, with respect to major utilities at least, to be an inviolable part of the post-war settlement prior to the privatization campaigns of the 1980s and 1990s. In some ways the 1950 Dorking agenda (that being the location of the Party's summit) had to await the New Labour agenda of the early 2000s to reach its logical culmination. For the moment it seemed essential for the Party to recognize that

> nationalisation had not turned out as the workers who had supported it had expected. The instruments of nationalisation had not worked their own loyalties and the workers had not yet found their proper place in industry ... The next step was to find, with the co-operation of the trade unions, ways in which the workers could become partners in each industry ... ways should be devised to put the nationalized industries on a basis of competitive rivalry.

If the newly nationalized industries presented a considerable challenge to Labour's democratic vision, the inhabitants of such represented an even greater one. Nowhere was Labour's democratic schizophrenia greater than in its dealings with the trades union movement. For the Party, of course, this was partly a problem of dealing with itself, its historical alter ego. It was, after all, largely created as a vehicle for the achievement of trades union Parliamentary and legislative ambitions. However much the Daltons and Jays, and before them the Webbs and others, and after them (though with greater ease in Party terms) the Blairs and Byers might distrust the representatives of the lower orders, they were financially and constitutionally in hock to the unions. It was not just that union finances were crucial to Party funds, particularly in the electoral cycle, or even that the trades union vote, wielded as ruthlessly at conference as institutional shareholders' own bloc votes in private corporations, it was even more that the unions were part of the body politic of Labour. Of the 393 Labour MPs elected in 1945, 119 were sponsored by trades unions (though not all would be trades unionists in any meaningful sense of the term), another 23 would be members of the Co-operative Party (most of whom would indeed be trades unionists). One assumes the ranks of the 49 lecturers and teachers, 44 lawyers, 25 journalists, 18 company directors and 15 doctors comprising the newly elected governing party were less specifically identifiable in trades union terms but trades union affiliations clearly provided the single largest organizational (if not always ideological) common denominator within the Parliamentary party.

As has already been seen, at moments of crisis, as in the power generating strikes, government could react by seeking to use the power of the state against strikers. At such moments government consistently examined the possibilities of enhancing the restrictions on trades unions' rights which had already been considerably curtailed as a wartime necessity – and many of those legislative restrictions remained in force throughout the government's tenure in office. It was, however, more than a question of localized or inevitable conflicts, more than a question even of the state, as the largest employer, becoming clearly (and publicly) embroiled in all sorts of industrial issues hitherto considered beyond its domain other than in times of national emergency. It was, above all, a question of the role of trades unions in the new social order. That concern was not confined to government representatives. As an article by J. R. Campbell (one-time author of *Direct Action* with Willie Gallacher, and, like Gallacher, a leading figure in the Communist Party of Great Britain) in *Labour Monthly* observed in September 1945,

> Of course the trade unionists must recognize the fact that they are operating in a controlled economy which is being steered by the Labour Government. They will have to consider the bearing of any wage policy which they put forward on the entire economic policy that the Government is pursuing ... the government can justly expect the union executives to do everything in their power to persuade members to work through the official machinery. It may be the tactic of certain employers to embarrass the Government by provoking strikes. Don't let us walk into this obvious trap by engaging in unofficial strikes ... Sabotage of the Labour Government may come not merely from the class-conscious employers but from the class-unconscious in the ranks of the workers.

Campbell's statist view of the proper function of trades unions and activists, and the terminal perils of false consciousness, did not long survive the onset of the Cold War. They did, however, have a long historical echo in Labour's governing circles. At times it is quite evident that, almost in a Brechtian sense, the government felt deeply betrayed by the workers and, if they could, would have preferred to elect another people who properly appreciated their efforts and their status as the embodiment of the national interest. Again Morrison voiced the ambition, wanting the workers 'to abandon the mentality of nineteenth-century capitalism', and to accept the new social order as an unrequited good.

In Party speak, the constant refrain was of the need to 'educate' the trades unions, even to the extent of establishing a Cabinet sub-committee 'to help with the problem of educating workers in the socialized industries in the purpose of socialisation'. While maintaining an 'educative' approach it was also deemed essential to maintain, and enhance, the pre-war secret emergency organization which had been established during the General Strike to provide state support during large-scale industrial disputes, and it was under these auspices that the government would, on a number of occasions, have recourse to the military to maintain what it deemed essential supplies or services. It was within that sphere, too, that government would maintain, and increase, surveillance on those deemed subversive by the security services, just as Harold Wilson would be kept abreast of the young John Prescott's activities as an industrial militant, and Barbara Castle be carefully informed of Hugh Scanlon's dalliances with undesirable elements. It was not just a question of alien subversives, it was a question of the right trades unionists – 'It is essential that the workers representatives should be men and women of sane outlook'. More than that, even, it was a question of the right type of trades unions. In many ways, from the perspective of government – particularly given the structure of the lobby/interest group state developed during and after the First World War – centralized government demanded centralized unions, and strong government demanded strong trades unions, so long as they were controlled by 'the right type'. As has been mentioned above, government frequently had recourse to trades unions, in particular to the trades unions representative/lobby body the Trades

Union Congress, to seek support for its policies and to control its members.

In this scenario it was never quite clear, and never could be quite clear, whether the governmental apparatus was meant to embrace trades union organizations as an administrative arm, a partner (however junior) in the affairs of state, or as representative organizations whose members' interests did not always coincide with those of the government. What was clear was that it was 'official' trades unions that were to be recognized, 'unofficial' ones (though under prevailing wartime legislations most disputes were necessarily 'unofficial') could only be construed as subversive. Strong unions in control of their members were therefore an unspoken assumption in policy making. In key areas, particularly nascent incomes policy (in the 1940s more correctly referred to as wages policy), government sought, usually secretly, to enlist TUC support. In ways which would prefigure the 1970s 'social contract' (and with about as much success), Cripps as Chancellor was willing to frame budgetary proposals in the context of TUC discussions so long as they secured acquiescence and allegiance.

It was Bevin, the seasoned trades union bruiser who opposed Cripps on the grounds, which would haunt successive Labour governments, that 'this would entail an inevitable clash between the workers and the government'. Time after time, however, with varying degrees of success, government reached for trades union assistance in smoothing the way for the implementation of what it considered would be unpopular policies. In the process, despite all its desires, it reinforced the tensions between shop floor and HQ, between officials and unofficial shop stewards and their like, which would characterize British industrial relations from the later 1950s to the early 1980s and beyond.

That, though, is a somewhat different story, albeit one which would have a significant impact not just on the trajectory of the future Labour Party, and its subsequent New Labour offspring which was clearly born with an institutionalized grudge against labour in any of its 'old' and organized forms. It is not to suggest that Labour's post-war administration was some kind of political aberration, still less to suggest it was an 'objective' (whatever that might be) failure. It is to suggest that, amidst all the real and desperate material pressures with which it had to deal, the democratic schizophrenia, the ingrained distrust of working-class organizations, the peculiarly British Parliamentary perspective ensured that the default position to which it retreated in moments of crisis – and it was constantly beset by crises – was exclusive rather than inclusive, and that, however new the social order might be, democratic forms were not to be a guiding priority.

Chapter 7

A Protracted Arc: Sex, Gender and Sexuality – Emancipation and Liberation

Gill Scott

Preamble

Any focus on the question of women and democracy at once presents us with the problematic implication that women are not already included in the great levelling concepts – natural rights, the people, the nation, the citizens – that buttress debates about governance, representation and social justice. And of course when we look into the origins and evolution of these terms we find that while they drew their moral and political legitimacy from their claim to universality and, therefore, their capacity to mobilize the many against the few, the tendency of their more particular usage has been the exclusion of sexual (as with racial, ethnic, and property-less) others. Historically, the contest for admission into the category of 'the people', and full membership of the political community, has been one of the main drivers of struggles for democracy. So it is to the claims of the female half of the human race in those struggles that we now turn.

The movement for the emancipation of women, like other great social movements for equality, has not advanced steadily or evenly. There have been high points and low points, stagnancy and reversals. For women in Britain, the aspiration to democratic participation has roots that can be traced back to early modern and even medieval instances of the utterances and actions of exceptional women and men, especially during the turbulence of the English Revolution. As a coherent set of demands, however, the female claim to citizenship, also known as the birth of feminism, is a distinctively modern phenomenon.

In all pre-modern societies of which we have reliable knowledge, the lives of women have been predominantly dictated by their biology; their reproductive capacities have given rise to varying degrees of dependence upon and subordination to men. A key development of modern history has been the process by which the situation of women, their powers and capacities, have ceased to appear as a natural necessity and become instead a question: what is the true nature of women and what, therefore, should be their proper place in society? Since the late eighteenth century, with the rise of industrial capitalism and the emergence of representative democracy, that question has been the subject of vigorous debate and contestation between feminists and anti-feminists. It has still not been fully resolved, and, in J. S. Mill's formulation, cannot be unless, or until, all discriminatory practices are eradicated.

Feminism's best-known early advocate is Mary Wollstonecraft. Her classic text, *Vindication of the Rights of Women* (1792), provides the first sustained argument in English for women's rights, and has never been out of print. In proposing that there was such a thing as women's rights (echoing French revolutionary tracts on '*les droites de la femme*'), Wollstonecraft went against the grain of religious, philosophical, legal and social certainties inscribed not only in the traditions of the *ancien régime* but in the writings of such enlightenment thinkers as Rousseau. Her priority was to establish that the capacities for knowledge, reason, morality and virtuous behaviour were human qualities possessed by individuals regardless of their sex; furthermore, if women did not always display such attributes, then it was the fault of their upbringing and circumstances not their nature. A virtuous society should take the necessary steps to ensure that all were in a position to obtain a character as a human being, regardless of sexual distinctions. Thus, through the even distribution of educational and employment opportunities, civil and political rights and responsibilities, women and men could share public and private space as good citizens.

All such formulations immediately pose the question of agency – how might change be brought about? Writing decades before anything resembling a women's movement existed, the only method available to Wollstonecraft was the art of persuasion through argument. Since her time, there have been two periods of intense activity in which feminism as an organized social and political movement as well as a body of ideas has sought to secure reforms in the interests of women and to challenge the verities of traditional masculine hegemony. First-wave feminism emerged in the mid-nineteenth century, peaked in the suffrage agitation of the early twentieth century and declined from the 1920s; second-wave feminism was born in the late 1960s, was at its height in the 1970s and lost momentum from the early 1980s.

It is difficult to quantify precisely the significance, or the net gains, of each of these periods in terms of democratic advances. On the one hand, landmark pieces of legislation have recognized, in principle, particular rights of women as necessary if not sufficient conditions of sexual equality; to take three obvious examples, to vote (1919 and 1928 Representation of the People Acts); to fertility control (1967 Abortion Act); to economic independence (1970 Equal Pay Act). The extent to which each of these correlates precisely with the pressure of organized feminism varies, but in every case there is undoubtedly a registration of important shifts having taken place in mainstream understanding about the powers, the capacities and the entitlements of women. And, on the other hand, through this more nebulous process of social and cultural transformation, the self-organization of women has made a huge, if less quantifiable, contribution. A great achievement of both feminist waves, in other words, has been, in deed and in word, and often in collaboration with male allies and comrades, the redefining and re-imagining of democratic aspirations.

First-Wave Feminism

First-wave feminism coincided, not accidentally, with a period of heightened activity in the labour movement and on the Left generally. As well as the steady expansion of education for women, economic growth and development, the intense suffrage campaigning in the decade before the First World War overlapped with and was fuelled by the rise of New Unionism in the late nineteenth century, the expansion of women's unions and other labour movement organizations, and the spread of socialism. In this militant atmosphere, the concept of emancipation, larger than simple enfranchisement, inspired a tremendous variety of initiatives on the rights and the wrongs of women, all underpinned by great confidence in the possibility of winning progressive change.

Much of what we now know about first-wave feminist activity is a product of second-wave feminism's project of uncovering what had been, in the words of Sheila Rowbotham's ground-breaking study, *Hidden from History* (1973). Yet for several decades, first-wave feminism, for contemporaries, simply the women's movement, was understood to have been synonymous with the struggle for the vote, the central focus of Ray Strachey's classic account, *The Cause* (1928), published in the year that women were finally enfranchised on equal terms with men. For six decades the demand for political rights inspired initiatives from a wide spectrum of political and social positions. The richly textured narratives of this struggle that are available to us range from the literally suicidal tactics of society ladies to the grinding determination of mill workers juggling the conflicting demands of activism, paid work and a home to run. The dramatic gestures of the militant suffragettes of the WSPU captured the attention of the press while to a great extent obscuring, for posterity as for contemporaries, the more prosaic but very varied efforts of the constitutionalists in the NUWSS. And the great unifying slogan of Votes for Women, at best, pulled together a broad church in which campaigners held very different views about the significance of the right to vote.

Politically and ideologically, the suffrage movement contained a multitude of differences and, often, divisions. The Pankhurst family, for example, with its ILP and trade-union roots, divided between Sylvia's revolutionary politics, expressed in the East London Suffrage Federation and her newspaper *The Dreadnought*, and Emmeline and Christabel's increasingly autocratic tendencies in the WSPU and then extreme right-wing sympathies. The shared goal of political rights could be widely interpreted. For some, it was about status and the need to remove a demeaning form of discrimination, an end in itself. For one such equal-rights feminist, the eventual winning of the vote in 1928 brought a particular kind of closure: 'I had money and freedom and the whole world to choose from', wrote Margaret Mackworth, Viscountess Rhondda. But for those concerned with women's emancipation and social equality, the vote was conceived as just one of a number of changes needed to secure justice for women.

To explore this emancipatory impulse, I want to turn to an organization whose work for women's advancement included support for the suffrage cause but was not limited by a narrow definition of political rights. The Women's Co-operative Guild (WCG)'s suffrage activity was considerable. At the national level, especially through its work in the People's Suffrage Federation, it played a key role in securing majority support in the Labour Party for women to be included in franchise reform; it was active in the local suffrage networks, and notably in the work of the northern working-class suffragists. Fundamentally, however, the Guild's political perspective was determined as much by its involvement with the working-class politics of the Co-operative movement as by its suffrage affiliations. Thus, the WCG saw the vote as a weapon for reform rather than an end in itself, and, importantly, did not wait for the vote to tackle the many 'grave injustices, hardships and miseries in women's lives'. By the eve of the First World War, with a membership of 30,000 women, the WCG, in its Citizenship work, was actively pursuing issues of concern to married women that in addition to the vote included campaigns for divorce law reform and for the provision of maternity benefit.

The WCG was in many ways an exceptional women's organization. Founded in 1883 to provide association and education for women in the British consumers' Co-operative movement, it was uniquely positioned to reach a social group that had previously been completely absent from public life – married women from the working class, specifically, the housewives who shopped at the Co-op stores. It did not come into being with explicitly feminist commitments – one of its early founders definitely ruled out the 'vex'd question of women's rights' – but it soon attracted a dynamic mixture of working-class activists and left-wing middle-class feminists, all of whom recognized the WCG's potential for bringing to working-class women the message of women's emancipation.

The careers of two of the weightiest figures in this process, Margaret Llewelyn Davies (1861–1944), and Sarah Reddish (1850–1928), reveal much about the politics of the WCG. Davies was the General Secretary of the WCG from 1889 to 1921. She remains a relatively obscure historical figure, largely by her own choice. Self-effacing and with an aversion to limelight, she destroyed most of her personal papers near the end of her life. But it is clear from the records of the WCG that its most radical initiatives bear her stamp. She came from a privileged but enlightened upper-middle-class background: her father, John Llewelyn Davies, was a Christian socialist, and pioneer of adult education; her aunt, Emily Davies, was a Victorian equal rights campaigner who founded the first Cambridge College for women, Girton. Well educated and with family support for her search for a socially worthwhile occupation, Davies was drawn to consumers' Co-operation because of its potential as an embryonic industrial democracy. She joined the Marylebone Co-operative Society, and then its fledgling women's organization, the WCG, which soon became, she later wrote, 'the pivot of my work'.

Davies's political priorities are evident in an early conference speech, urging members to take up such questions as women's suffrage and trade unionism. The 1890 pamphlet *How to Start and Work a Branch* is a kind of mission statement for the Guild:

> Working women are now beginning to find out, as men have done, that
> the means for improving their conditions and redressing their wrongs lie

largely in their own hands. Some privileges have belonged too exclusively to one sex; other privileges too exclusively to one class. It is high time that, as far as possible, all that makes a life most happy and fruitful should be brought within the reach of all.

In the year Davies became General Secretary of the WCG, 1889, her family left London for Westmorland after her father, who had been Rector of Christ Church, Marylebone, with expectations of gaining a bishopric, delivered a 'blistering attack on imperialism' in a sermon before Queen Victoria and then retreated to the provinces. Significantly for the WCG, this move brought its Head Office closer to a new constituency: working women of the mill towns of Lancashire and Cheshire. This was the heart of the Co-operative movement, home of the first Co-operative Society, the Rochdale Pioneers founded in 1844, and, importantly, with a vibrant tradition of female trade unionism. This was fertile soil for the WCG. In 1889, the organization had 7 of its 50 branches in the north; ten years later, the North Western Section accounted for a 100 of total of 262 branches, and 6,600 of its 12,537 members.

The move north brought Davies into contact with an important new ally in building the Guild. Sarah Reddish was a working-class woman of formidable talents and energies, one of the emerging new breed of female political activists. The daughter of a prominent Bolton Co-operator – the honorary librarian and secretary of Bolton Society – she worked in the textile industry from the age of 11, joined the Guild in the 1880s, was involved in women's trade unionism, and became a leading radical suffragist, prominent in the North of England Society for Women's Suffrage. In 1901 she led a deputation to the House of Commons that presented the Lancashire female textile workers' petition of almost 30,000 signatures. She was also active in municipal politics, and in 1900 won a seat on Bolton School Board with 12,418 votes, coming sixth out of 18 candidates.

When Davies first met her, Reddish was President of the flourishing Bolton Women's Guild and a member of the Guild Central Committee. From 1893 to 1895 she was employed as the Guild's first full-time paid organizer. In 1893, Reddish described a visit to the

General Secretary at the Kirkby Lonsdale Rectory, and her introduction to the guild office and 'letters, papers, and work almost
unlimited in amount'. Reddish played a key role in Davies's political
education. At Reddish's death in 1928, Davies paid tribute to her old
friend, 'whose life was devoted to the causes of women and labour',
and remembered sitting over the fire at the Kirkby Lonsdale rectory
while Reddish dwelt upon 'the large Socialistic vision of a new life
which filled her mind'.

It is apparent that Reddish shared Davies's determination to hold
the politics of sex and of class in balance. Her 1894 Organizer's
Report illustrates the kinds of arguments she was developing to
convince sex-prejudiced Co-operative officials of the entitlement of
the WCG to a share of Co-operative funds. 'We are told by some,'
she wrote, 'that women are wives and mothers, and that the duties
therein involved are enough for them. We reply, that men are
husbands and fathers, and that they, as such, have duties not to be
neglected, but we join in the general opinion that men should also
be interested in the science of government, taking a share in the
larger family of the store, the municipality and the State. The WCG
has done much towards impressing the fact that women as citizens
should take their share in this work also.'

So already, in the 1890s, the WCG was opening a space for active
citizenship for women from working-class backgrounds, often with
little formal education. One such member was Mrs Bury, a former
mill worker and housewife in her 40s. She described the 1893 Guild
Conference in Leicester as 'a revelation'. On each of the three days of
the gathering, she wrote,

> my vision seemed to be widening, and my spirit felt that here was the
> very opportunity I had always been seeking, but never put into words. I
> had longings and aspirations and a vague sense of power within myself
> which had never had an opportunity for realisation. At the close of the
> meetings I felt as I imagine a war-horse must feel when he hears the beat
> of a drum.

Yet as well as providing unprecedented opportunities for women
such as Mrs Bury to play a public role, the WCG was also becoming

the means by which the demand for justice was applied to the domestic sphere. The General Secretary, regularly visiting branches and staying in members' homes, was constantly impressed, as she wrote in 1899, by the 'great capacity – the practical wisdom and public spirit – which the guild is bringing out and turning to valuable account'. But greater familiarity with the lives of working women was a double-edged process. From a relatively sheltered background, Davies was also moved and shocked by the grimness, the hardship and the narrowness of women's lives that she witnessed; as she put it, the 'struggles with want', 'constant ill health; unselfish devotion rewarded by lack of consideration'.

What emerges from the Guild's early development is a sense of married working-class women having agency – the capacity to organize and to effect change, on the one hand, but also of suffering particular forms of oppression. In 1907, these insights found expression in a feminist analysis of the situation of married women provided in a Guild discussion paper by Rosalind Nash, *The Position of Married Women*. Nash noted that in 1869, John Stuart Mill had described the wife as the 'bond-servant of her husband'. Since then, she continued, 'we might say that they have been promoted from slaves to servants' – but with the important qualification that while a servant could ask for better wages and conditions to compensate for living-in, a wife could not bargain with her husband over her home and her children. Slowly, the idea had gained ground that married woman were entitled to more than a life of drudgery but without some intervention by the women themselves, progress would be slow. Their main problem was their isolation: it is difficult, she pointed out, 'for each woman separately to assert herself against the unjust claims of home'. So here was an opportunity for collective action: 'the Guild can be a kind of trade union, through which ... we can spread better ideas.'

Meanwhile, the vote would surely be a weapon in tackling the many problems of their lives. The wife would gain formal recognition as a joint head of the family and as a citizen with rights and responsibilities. There was also scope for legislation to be brought forward to secure changes which would entitle her to a share of the family income, make decisions concerning her children, and perhaps challenge the 'repulsive' divorce laws that at present made it so difficult for her to leave a cruel husband. And here, Mrs Nash provided anecdotal evidence of the brutish treatment of married women, adding dryly that is was only through 'such glimpses that we can get an idea of what goes on in some homes, for of course, the privacy of the home is sacred'.

In 1910, the WCG found an opportunity publicly to challenge the conventionally 'sacred' privacy of the home when, in recognition of its status as an organization of some 25,000 Co-operative women, it was invited to give evidence to the Royal Commission on Divorce and Matrimonial Causes. Under the terms of existing legislation, only the rich could afford divorce proceedings – poorer people could only have legal separation without the possibility of marrying again. For those who could afford divorce, the law enshrined a sexual double standard whereby a husband could divorce his wife for an act of adultery while a wife had to prove a cause in addition to adultery.

In the WCG's deliberations on this subject, it generated what are arguably the most critical feminist positions of the era. It is hard now to recapture how taboo a subject divorce then was. Mindful of the stigma attached to the very idea of a failed marriage, the Guild leadership moved cautiously. At the 1910 Congress, with over 500 delegates present, expecting conflicting opinions, a senior guildswoman moved a resolution condemning the sexual inequality of the existing divorce laws and calling for cheaper proceedings. She made 'a weighty and restrained speech, with a grave sense of the difficulty and responsibility of her task'. She was seconded by a midwife who 'spoke from intimate personal knowledge of the lives of women. The audience listened with great attention and a discussion was fully anticipated'. But 'not a single delegate rose to speak. They were prepared to vote instantly'. A 'forest of hands showed itself immediately and silently. There were only five raised against it.' Here was emphatic evidence that working women, often supposed to be the group most in need of the protection of unbreakable marriage vows, wanted, as one journalist put it, 'cheap and easy divorce'.

The Guild then collected written statements, in the form of 131 letters, from members giving explicit and intimate details of marriage and childbirth that were submitted as evidence to the Commission. Their content helps to explain why divorce elicited greater 'strength and earnestness of feeling' than any other subject in the Guild's history. Nearly every woman had first- or second-hand knowledge of the 'hidden suffering' endured within failed marriages. The most shocking cases described violence, marital rape, forced miscarriage and abortion: evidence that the great mass of the suffering was borne by women. No woman, Davies observed, 'could inflict on a man the amount of degradation that a man may force on a woman'.

'My cousin', wrote one member, 'married a man who has behaved most brutally towards her, has broken her teeth, blacked her eyes, and bruised her body, and I believe is not kind to the children ... he has killed every spark of love she had for him, but she must put up for the children's sake.' Another described women who always tried to induce an abortion on discovering that they were pregnant, because 'the husband will grumble and make things unpleasant, because there will be another mouth to fill and he may have to deprive himself of something'. In another case, the husband 'always thrashes his wife and has put her life in danger in his anger on discovering her condition'.

This material made a great impression on the liberal-minded members of the Commission, and its majority recommendations were broadly in line with those of the Guild. But the immediate passing of legislation was interrupted by the war, and it is a measure of the advanced nature of the reforms proposed that they did not become law until the 1960s; marital rape was not legally recognized until 1991.

What the Guild was doing in this early period, however, was claiming the authority to give voice to the experience and the interests of a previously silent and concealed community of women, urging their right not only to vote but to be treated with greater respect as wives and mothers. All this exposed the hypocrisy of Victorian domestic ideology. As Davies put it:

It seemed as if in the past, when women married, they retired behind a dark curtain on which was embroidered all sorts of beautiful sentiments about the beauty of motherhood and the sanctity of the home; but now the curtain was being withdrawn, and from the discussion that had taken place they had learned much of the sufferings of married women, the pain and misery that were going on behind the curtain.

It was, she conceded,

perhaps inevitable that the mother should have been publicly overlooked, for the isolation of women in married life has, up to now, prevented any common expression of their needs. They have been hidden behind the curtain which falls after marriage, the curtain which women are now themselves raising.

The great achievement of the WCG then was to bring into organizational life a previously silent and invisible constituency – married women of the working class, and to evolve a political agenda that began to express their needs. In 1913, when it had 30,000 members, the Russian social democrat, Alexandra Kollontai, was a guest speaker at one of its regional conferences. What especially struck her about the Guild was that 'it was always said that factory women could be politicized but housewives, never – they could never get outside their homes.' Now the Guild was proving this wrong and she wanted to see it represented at international socialist gatherings.

The WCG's highly distinctive contribution to feminism was organizational but also conceptual. It was through the growth and development of the Guild itself that what Davies termed the 'hidden suffering' of women in married life was brought to light, and the agency to contest this form of oppression brought into being. To build a kind of trade union for married women, and to begin to promote their interests as a particular constituency, was by any measure an outstanding achievement. It did not happen by accident. The Guild's vigour in this early period rested on three exceptional features: an organizational structure that combined rank and file democracy and a progressive leadership; the conviction that women needed their own affiliated but autonomous organizations within the wider working-class movement, and should control their own policy in that space; a willingness to bring a feminist analysis to bear on the situation of women within the working-class family. Through its campaigning work, the WCG made a small mark in the public domain to the effect that freedom for women required their empowerment in the domestic sphere as well as in civic life. In this the Guild's work anticipated some of the big issues of second-wave feminism, issues that were, in the intervening half a century years and for complex reasons, closed down.

Second-wave feminism

Feminism did not entirely evaporate between the 1920s and the 1960s, but through political marginalization and incremental failures of renewal, contracted to a point where it needed reinvention. In time, the second-wave feminist movement that emerged in the late 1960s was to discover continuities and communities of interest in the past. In the moment, however, a new generation of activists experienced themselves as without precedent and with a wholly new agenda for change.

In important ways, their perception was correct. The historical and political context of the Women's Liberation Movement (WLM) endowed it not only with an acute appreciation of injustice but also an immense capacity for imagining progress. Firstly, it was nourished by the post-war economic boom. In the West, a quarter of a century of sustained economic growth, full employment, and rising living standards fed into a great sense of optimism that social problems and inequality could be eradicated. Secondly, and riding on the crest of this wave, with the expansion of higher education and cost-of-living indexed grants, was the birth of student radicalism and the emergence of the New Left and attendant protest movements: against nuclear arms and the war in Vietnam, for black civil rights in the USA; links with trade unions; direct action in the Universities themselves.

Thirdly, and overlapping with the political militancy of the protest movements, was the so-called sexual revolution. Starting in the USA and spreading across the Atlantic, the counterculture brought a libertarian shaking up of traditional sexual morality, converging in Britain, with progressive legislation and social innovation that included the legalisation of abortion, the widening availability of the contraceptive pill, and the reform of the divorce laws to admit grounds of mutual incompatibility, with an equal share of assets for the wife. With the law, medical science and social policy combining to make it possible to detach sexual pleasure from the risk of pregnancy, and to escape an unhappy marriage without complete impoverishment and social stigma, what had, despite the winning of the vote and other formal rights, remained destiny for most women – marriage and motherhood – now for the first time in history started to become an option.

These trends underpinned WLM in complex and contradictory ways. Women were indivisibly part of an expanding economy and a changing labour market, as they were caught up in the counter-culture and the sexual revolution. In all these areas, however, their involvement was heavily gendered. Workplaces, colleges, and even radical groupings, were all ingrained with traditional practices and values about femininity – the proper roles and responsibilities of women – that still firmly centred them in the domestic sphere. Prevailing assumptions about marriage and motherhood in practice restricted women's educational and employment opportunities; the young women who joined the protest movements generally found themselves making tea and typing leaflets; the permissive values of the counterculture put new pressures on women to conform to male expectations of them as sex objects.

What was going on in the 1960s was not so much an intensification of women's oppression, although the emerging mass-consumer society did generate demeaning new stereotypes, as a deepening frustration on the part of many young women at the gap between expectations and reality. Critically, the counterculture offered powerful models and openings for intervention to secure change. So, in the turmoil of new political experiences and lifestyle experiments, it is not surprising that the initiative on women's issues came from the politically experienced activists of the protest movements. In Britain, as in the USA, it was, for the greater part, young women who had gained analytical and organizational skills from, for example, civil rights, CND, and the socialist groupings of the New Left, who began to formulate a critique of women's situation and demands on behalf of their sex.

Their sense of being caught up in a wholly new enterprise is evident in their early exploration, often in consciousness raising groups (that drew on the concept of black consciousness raising), of a problem with no name. As this problem was investigated and theorized in a series of texts (Juliet Mitchell, *Women's Estate* (1971), Germaine Greer, *The Female Eunuch* (1970), Shulamith Firestone, *The Dialectic of Sex* (1970)), more traditional feminist arguments for equality in actually existing society converged with the idea of Liberation – a larger, more universal vision of social transformation in which not only women but the whole of humanity would achieve its full potential.

So the concerns and ambitions of the WLM were thus more sweeping and far-reaching than those of its predecessors. This sense of boundlessness is apparent in its organizational form, not tightly structured with a formal constitution and membership lists but, by the early 1970s, and echoing developments in the USA, a loose network of local women's groups in different cities, towns and neighbourhoods. Basic demands were drawn up, underpinned by the assumptions that economic equality through paid work was indispensable for true equality; that there should be no form of sexual discrimination in education, training and employment; that these opportunities should be available for all women regardless of their marital status and whether or not they had children; that the welfare state should provide comprehensive childcare facilities; that medical science should enable women to plan pregnancies so that every child would be wanted and every mother willing; that the law and society more generally should guarantee freedom from discrimination on grounds of sex or sexuality and put an end to male aggression against women. This agenda reflected the con-fidence and optimism of the times – the belief in continued economic growth and the ever-more egalitarian expansion of the welfare state – alongside a vision of democratic social transformation that, however utopian it might appear it retrospect, at the time seemed sufficiently credible to win the active participation of hundreds of thousands of women.

The formal aims of WLM, furthermore, never fully expressed the range of its concerns and activities. In its heyday, this fusion of political and cultural energy engendered breadth and depth of vision, and a desire for transformation that went deeper than any ideology, implying, as Sheila Rowbotham puts it, a psychological break with all that had gone before. For many active feminists, there was a commitment to change that entailed living your politics, changing your whole outlook and lifestyle. The WLM was not in power: its demands were not going to be implemented in the immediate future but the strength of the movement came from the belief that the process of change could be helped along through a variety of initiatives. Feminists set up reading groups, street theatre, musicians' and writers' workshops; they lived in women's houses, held women's discos, organized fundraising events; they produced newsletters and a national glossy magazine, *Spare Rib*, opened bookshops and launched publishing houses, such as Virago and The Women's Press. And they inaugurated women's studies, later gender studies, in virtually all branches of academia.

The network of women's groups around the country took up a multitude of campaigns and different forms of direct action. They targeted the local state, the national state, educational and legal policies, trade unions and the media. They campaigned for abortion rights, women's health care, better training and conditions of service for women workers, workplace crèches, pre-school nurseries. They took initiatives on sex education for young women, the establishment of Rape Crisis Centres, and Battered Wives' Refuges. They made contact with tenants' groups, community groups and trade unionists; the close links with the labour movement were evident in 1978 in a 100,000-strong National Abortion Campaign march sponsored by the TUC.

Yet for all its energy and innovation, the grand vision of Women's Liberation has not been fulfilled. What is its legacy? It is not the case that in failing to fulfil its promise, WLM achieved nothing. Even the most cursory comparison of mainstream representations of femininity in the 1970s with those of the 2000s reveals that an enormous cultural transformation has taken place in attitudes and expectations about women's lives. Subjects that have enormous significance for women but were virtually unmentionable three decades ago, such as domestic violence, abortion and mastectomy, now have a place in public discourse. Few people do not understand the concept of sexism. Corporations and institutions have to have a position on equal opportunities. It is commonplace for industrial tribunals to take up cases of sex discrimination.

But politically, the steady decline and internal divisions of the WLM since the 1970s have been indivisible from the rise of Thatcherism, Blairism and the triumph of market forces and globalization. Without the ballast of a militant labour movement, a robust Left and Keynesian economic orthodoxies, feminist theory has retreated to increasingly obscure debates within the academy while feminist practice has been spread thinly over a range of diverse and often incompatible equal opportunities initiatives. The growing gap between successful high earners and the marginal poor has underscored the inability of feminism pure and simple to speak for all women. The ambitious and well-qualified women who encounter glass ceilings in corporate career structures and sexual harassment on the trading floor are already benefiting from the services of typically low-paid cleaners and child carers. In the 1970s the WLM made a very serious assault on dominant ideologies of gender, in particular the mainstream sexual objectification of women. Today there is a striking absence of critical debate about such matters as the proliferation of make-over shows that service an expanding cosmetic surgery industry.

Conclusion

So what have this micro-study of the WCG and macro-study of WLM to tell us about women and democracy?

In both cases, we find exceptional instances of collectives of women intervening to shape their destiny and to create more democratic societies. In both cases, the process was as important as the envisaged outcomes, and appeared, for some years, to possess a self-sustaining momentum. Their visions were shaped by what was possible in their times – developments in productive labour, medical science, employment practices and the technology of labour-saving devices all contributed to this during the twentieth century, creating possibilities not available to the WCG – but the need to provide for the health, well-being and dignity of all women was the common thread.

In both cases, the convention, common to both liberal and socialist discourses about democracy, to focus on the public sphere was challenged by a concern with the politics of the domestic sphere. Davies called it the lifting of the curtain; an early WLM poster depicted Jenny serving Karl his dinner with the words: Parity Begins At Home. In both cases, this investigation of the domestic sphere opened a debate about the politics of reproductive rights. Again, the content was determined by what was possible at the time but in both cases there was an insistence on a woman's right to her body.

In both cases, a particular synthesis of the politics of class and the politics of gender, what Ellen Du Bois calls working at the hyphen, generated an organizational and rhetorical capacity to be inclusive, and to add substance to the claim, always inscribed in feminism but not always borne out, to speak for all women. In the early development of the WCG, and in WLM in the 1970s, there was attention to the needs and to the particular involvement of working-class women.

In both cases, the vision, the energy and the confidence of these collectives of women came not simply from their feminist commitments but from the soil in which they were rooted – specific historical moments of a strong Left, and a vigorous working-class movement. Equally, in both cases, those were circumstances that made it possible for those women to develop their own 'affiliated but autonomous movements'.

Reflecting on these high points of feminist activity, it is impossible to avoid the question of their relationship to formal representation in the British parliamentary system. It is without doubt the case that the advancement of women's legal position in society, the rights and entitlements that can be claimed, was dependent on the enactment of legislation, and, therefore, on the securing of a parliamentary majority in favour of those changes. Yet it is equally impossible to ignore the fact that, in the case of every such gain, including the vote itself, it was parliament that had to be dragged reluctantly to the concession. Only after the event, sometimes long after the event, did all and sundry, from left and from right, claim credit for the progress made. Wherein, therefore, does democracy reside? In the case of the legislative gains secured in women's favour, it would be hard not to conclude that in the absence of extra-parliamentary initiatives – agitation, organization, demonstration – there would have been anything more than pious parliamentary eloquence from the legislature and its executive incumbents. And in pivotal moments of feminist struggle that hinged on legislative processes, whether applying pressure for enfranchisement or defending abortion rights, the balance of forces has shifted most decisively when the critical mass of feminist organization, including working-class women, has been able to rouse the support of the labour movement.

Chapter 8

Democracy – the Long Revolution

Tony Benn in conversation with David Powell

> *Continuity in government represents no real need of national safety but merely a closing up of the ranks of the governing classes against their common enemy: the people. Ever since 1832, the upper classes of England have been faced with retaining as much of the substance of power whilst abandoning their forms to the clamour of democrats.*
>
> Bertrand Russell, *The Practice and Theory of Bolshevism*, 1920

Thirty years have passed since Lord Hailsham warned of the emerging dangers of 'an elective dictatorship'. A Parliamentary veteran who served as Lord Chancellor in three successive Tory administrations, Hailsham knew what he was about. At the time, however, he was widely dismissed as a Jeremiah. No longer. In the past three decades his fears have gained in substance. The evidence is there for all to see. On the one hand, there is the growing con-centration of power in the hands of the executive; on the other, there is the progressive erosion of our civil liberties.

Of course, the word democracy defies exact definition. Its very ambiguity, in fact, is both its strength and its weakness: its strength for the vision it inspires; its weakness for its exploitation by those who call it up to disguise their own ambitions, to secure their own hegemony. For Edmund Burke, democracy was: 'the most shameless thing in the world', while for the poet Walt Whitman it remained 'the password primeval'.

And it is here where the danger lies. We may flatter ourselves that our Constitution and civil liberties are sacrosanct, inviolate ... If so, we are fooling ourselves. History tells us otherwise: the mid-twentieth-century instances of Germany and Spain and Italy, to name but a few, are not to be dismissed as mere aberrant examples. All, at least nominally, were democracies. Each, in their turn, collapsed into fascism.

Of course, the temptation is to say, 'That's all very well, but it couldn't happen here', and adopt the complacent assumption that authoritarianism in all its guises is fundamentally alien to the British political culture. I am old enough, however, to remember Mosley's black shirts strutting the streets of London, and hearing of how a 1934 rally of the British Union of Fascists attracted an audience of 12,000 activists.

No question, the conditions then were very different from now. Fascism represented a coup against democracy that was evident for all to see, Mussolini going so far as to boast that he had buried democracy for a hundred years. Then the assault was overt, explicit, clearly defined. But what if it was altogether more covert, more subtle; a gradual and piecemeal erosion of our liberties and rights? What then? Could Hailsham's 'elective dictatorship' be realized by stealth rather than by force? Could we be deprived our rights and liberties without even realising what we have lost? Possibly not, but it would be foolish to pretend that the possibility does not exist.

If so, if there is a danger of such a situation arising, the problem is to define its character, to examine the complexities of establishment power, economic and political, and to determine whether such a situation might be the product of accident or design. Clearly, the character of the establishment has changed significantly since Bertrand Russell warned of the threat to democracy over 80 years ago.

Traditionally the term referred to the Monarchy, the Lords and Commons, the grandees of the shires and, more recently, to the industrial magnates who emerged in the nineteenth century – all underwritten by their agents, the capital markets of the City of London. While everything changes, however, everything remains much the same. The City and Westminster continue to represent, exactly, the polarities of power – political and economic.

It was a combination of which the economic historian R. H. Tawney wrote in 1938:

> Our political institutions are, on the whole, a source of pride. Our economic institutions and the social system based on them ought to be the same; in fact, they are not ... Democracy is unstable as a political system as long as it remains a political system and little more.

The same remains true, a commentary on the timeless contest between political and economic power. Since Tawney wrote, however, globalization and the growth of multi-national corporations have progressively shifted the balance of power in favour of Capital, which may account for New Labour's conviction that there was no way of bucking the market, and its decision to work closely with the City and big business. Whether or not that does something to explain the shift in the balance of power in Westminster, and the widely held view that we are moving, inexorably, to an executive style of government remains open to debate. One thing, however, is clear: that since Hailsham delivered his Dimbleby Lecture in 1976, both Cabinet and Parliamentary powers have been progressively eroded at the expense both of the constitution and our civil liberties. Indeed, the one cannot be divorced from the other, as the Iraq débâcle revealed.

In synthesis, the second Gulf War highlighted, precisely, the new compact of power. In the global context, it revealed much about the nature of Britain's 'special relationship' with the United States, and the role of the trans-nationals, more especially the oil companies, in the political decision-taking process. In the national context, it revealed much about the subordination of Parliament to what might well be termed 'command politics', and the orchestration of public fears in an attempt by government to drive through punitive legislation, contemptuous of the judiciary.

The information that has come out since the end of the second Gulf War, information only grudgingly released by the government, reveals as much about the inner workings of executive power as it does about how No. 10 was willing to economize with the truth in order to achieve its ends. As early as September, 2002, seven months before the invasion of Iraq, and shortly after he had held a meeting with George Bush at his ranch in Texas, Blair summoned what amounted to a council of war with his closest advisers. Apparently, Bush had made it plain that he intended to invade Iraq and replace Saddam Hussein, a decision which led the then head of MI6, Sir Richard Dearlove, to assert that 'the intelligence and facts were being fixed around the policy'.

Blair, however, was already aware of the Foreign Office's reservations about the use of force to achieve a regime change in Baghdad. Before his meeting with Bush, Elizabeth Wilmshurst, the FO's deputy legal adviser, had been party to preparing a confidential memorandum which listed many of the reservations that were later to feature prominently in the Attorney General, Lord Goldsmith's, advice to No. 10 on the legality of using force to achieve a regime change in Iraq. Submitted on 7 March 2003, the 13-page document expressed serious reservations about committing Britain to war – a war based on highly suspect intelligence reports that had been exaggerated to justify the policies that Bush and Blair were bent on pursuing.

And what of the Cabinet and Parliament all this while? What role did they play in what, arguably, is the most crucial decision any government can take: committing Britain to war? The answer is clear. Virtually none. True, Blair could have ridden roughshod over both the Cabinet and Parliament, and called on Royal prerogative to underwrite his decision. He didn't, preferring, instead, to circulate a highly abbreviated, one-page summary of Goldsmith's advice to the Cabinet on 17 March – a position paper from which Goldsmith's caveats had been carefully excised.

Twenty-four hours later, the Leader of the House, and former Foreign Secretary, Robin Cook, resigned. He did so to challenge Blair's claim that Iraq possessed weapons of mass destruction, and to declare, 'It has been a favourite theme of commentators that this House no longer occupies a central role in British politics. Nothing could better demonstrate that they are wrong than for the House to stop the commitment of troops to a war that has neither international agreement nor domestic support.'

It made no difference. Seventy-two hours later, Britain was at war. The subsequent Hutton and Butler enquiries, the first into the death of the government scientist, David Kelly, the second into the use made by government of 'sexed up' intelligence, only lifted a corner of the curtain cloaking the prelude to the war. Two years were to pass, however, between the outbreak of hostilities and the publication of full details of how the Prime Minister had deceived Parliament and the public in order to achieve his own, and George Bush's, ends. These were revelations that prompted a leading jurist, Philippe Sands, to declare that Blair's practice of playing fast and loose with the Attorney General's advice, 'raises concerns of the greatest constitutional significance'.

Betty Boothroyd, until 2001 Speaker of the Commons, had long been expressing much the same concern. Within two months of New Labour taking power in May 1997, she was warning government that it was the role of Parliament to hold the executive to account, a criticism she was to repeat in July 1998, 'I cannot deprecate strongly enough the leaks and briefings that go on behind our backs'. She was to repeat the charge in December of the same year, 'What is happening is that this House and the status of this House is being devalued, and I deprecate it most strongly', and reiterate the point yet again following her retirement, 'I wanted the Commons to be the centre of democratic debate in our country, not an adjunct of the *Today* programme or an echo chamber for party spin doctors.'

The government remained deaf to what it did not wish to hear. Not that such concerns are limited to the growing concentration of executive power, and the marginalizing of the legislature. The reverse. If serious questions were raised about the legality of the war then, as a by product, equally serious questions were asked about the erosion of the rule of law, and the marginalizing of the judiciary. Prompted by the fear of terrorism, and disregarding fears about the threat to civil liberties, the government fast tracked a series of increasingly punitive measures, to announce the suspension of the rights of suspected terrorists, and preventing the publication of the names of such detainees, or the nature of the evidence of the charges against them. And all this when there were already 200 pieces of anti-terrorist legislation on the statute books.

Piecemeal, the carefully woven fabric of civil liberty is being unravelled, to flout the principles that have remained the touchstone of civil law since the signing of Magna Carta in 1215: 'No freeman shall be arrested or detained, in prison or deprived of his freehold or outlawed or exiled or in any way molested ... except by the lawful judgement of his peers.' It was defence of Magna Carta that prompted the Law Lords to mount a scathing attack on the indefinite detention of sixteen foreign terrorist suspects without trial, leading Lord Hoffmann to warn that, 'The real threat to the life of the nation ... comes not from terrorism but laws such as these', and Lord Scott to declare, 'Indefinite imprisonment ... on grounds not disclosed is the stuff of nightmares, associated whether accurately or inaccurately with Soviet Russia in the Stalinist era and now with the U.K.'

The government was quick to respond by introducing revised legislation extending the Home Office's powers providing for the house arrest of British citizens, as well as foreigners, on the say so of ministers. Yet again the right to a fair trial, the presumption of innocence until found guilty, and to the principle that no citizen can have his or her freedom imperilled by the arbitrary power of the state was under threat. And yet again, the Lords tempered the proposed measures. That did little, however, to disguise the mindset of a government apparently hell-bent on overriding the rule of law.

The irony is inescapable. Long regarded as the twin agents of establishment power, it is the judiciary and the Lords who now occupy the last line of defence of our civil liberties.

As for myself, I never thought that Magna Carta would be denounced as 'Old Labour'. Indeed, if the anti-terrorism measures now on the statute books are applied in practice, they could equally well be directed against the trade unions, the animal liberation front, Greenpeace, or to virtually anyone who dares to challenge a government decree. In short, what we are talking about is a virtually limitless extension of executive power, so that any future PM will be able to use such measures to imprison whoever they like. Clearly, it is a deadly threat, and all in the name of what Blair declared to be 'a war for democracy'. The epigram had a familiar ring. Shortly after VE Day, 1945, Churchill called it up in a speech in the Commons, to insist that the credit for victory lay as much with British institutions as with British arms, more especially 'the democratic constitution' that had enabled Parliament to 'rest safely and solidly upon the will of the British people'.

The contrast between then and now is revealing, not least for what it says in the shift in the balance of power. Of course, it is nonsense to pretend that the democratic constitution that Churchill idealized was, itself, ideal. We had not, either then or now, by any means completed the democratic process begun in the seventeenth century. Far from it. What is clear, however, is that in the last three decades, the whole process has been thrown into reverse, for both the definition and the practice to be subverted. The question is: how has this come about? Exactly what factors and forces have been in play to account for the erosion of the constitution, albeit an unwritten one, with all that this implies? How is it that our parliamentary democracy now finds itself with an elective monarch – the Prime Minister – who uses powers notionally vested in the Crown, to bypass the legislature?

Seventy years ago I heard King Edward VIII's abdication broadcast, and learned the most important lesson about the British system of government: that the establishment regarded the crown as central to the defence of its power and privileges, and was not prepared to put the monarchy at risk by allowing the King to marry a divorced woman, Mrs Simpson, or to become so controversial as to threaten the myth that the monarchy was above politics. We claim that this country is a democracy but the Queen always refers to Britain as a constitutional monarchy because, technically, she summons and dissolves Parliament, and approves the composition of her governments. Meanwhile, every MP has to swear an oath of allegiance, and royal assent is required before any Bill becomes an Act of Parliament.

And this is not all. By calling up prerogatives, the executive, in the name of the Crown, has the power to declare war, to sign treaties, to create peers, and to appoint archbishops and bishops, each of whom has to declare his homage: 'that your majesty is the only supreme governor of this your realm.' A piece of medieval claptrap which remains a key prop of the executive, the net effect being that whereas democracy was the idea that you elected people to control the economy in the interests of the electorate, the executive now controls the electorate in the interests of the economy. That such power continues to exist beggars belief, the more so when reinforced by a host of unelected and, consequently, unaccountable advisers who play the same role as the Privy Council once did when Britain was governed by an absolute monarchy. Agents of the new as opposed to the old establishment, their numbers have grown exponentially over the past 10 years, effectively to supplant the role of senior civil servants who, themselves, were once formidable members of the establishment. A certain resentment may have triggered the claim of a former Permanent Secretary, Sir Christopher Foster, that Blair has carried change in constitutional practice to the point of revolution by politicizing the bureaucracy and crushing its independence.

The TV series *Yes Minister* may have guyed the role of the mandarins of Whitehall, and during my own time in office I didn't always find my Permanent Secretaries the easiest of people to deal with. They could be awkward, contumacious, many things. Nonetheless, as neutral, but far from neutered, censors their role in shaping and implementing policy, they were subject always to ministerial control, and to parliamentary scrutiny. This principle was central to the working of government. And now? The Hutton and Butler enquiries exposed the shift in power which has resulted in a growing resemblance to a presidential style of government, lacking in openness, and limiting the checks and balances on executive power.

As for the Cabinet, Blair has turned Harold Wilson's precept, 'Cabinet is a democracy not an autocracy', on its head. When it came to reaching major policy decisions, Wilson's cabinet meetings would last for several hours. The discussions were often abrasive, hard fought, as in the 1974 case of whether or not a referendum should be held on Britain's entry into the Common Market. The contrast with present practice is as instructive as it is disturbing for what it reveals about the aggrandizement of the executive. Today we are told that the Cabinet normally meets for about half an hour, when Blair tells them what he has decided, based on a series of bilateral meetings with Ministers. Indeed, in the case of the Iraq débâcle, the full Cabinet was only briefed on the invasion plans 72 hours before war was declared – and then only on the basis of the (abbreviated) advice provided by the Attorney General.

But that is not altogether surprising. As far back as 1995, Blair's pollster Philip, now Lord, Gould was calling for 'a unitary command structure' in the Party, leading straight to the leader, and a 'new culture' with the leader as 'the ultimate source of all authority'. Careless of the charge that Gould's formula smacked of Leninism – a charge that Gould himself echoed: 'I think that in periods of change a little bit of Leninism goes a long way' – the New Labour hierarchy was bent on securing absolute control of the Party, and, if elected, the legislature.

New Labour's overwhelming, and virtually unprecedented, majorities in 1997 and 2001 reinforced rather than restrained this drive to centralize power. Cautiously at first, but with increasing confidence, the Party machine proceeded to strip constituencies of their powers, and to substitute focus groups for open debate; it acted to cull potential dissenters, and to provide local parties with cherry-picked lists from which to select their Parliamentary candidates; it succeeded in converting the Party Conference into a rally for the leadership, and in deploying the National Policy Forum (designed to oversee policy development, and composed largely of New Labour placemen) to prevent contentious issues coming before Conference.

Inexorably, the ability to question the 'ultimate source of authority' was whipped out of the Party. And where the whip failed, there was always the carrot of patronage. George Bernard Shaw was right, 'Getting patronage is the whole art of life. A man cannot have a career without it.' Of course, 'the old corruption' has always been a tool of government, and applies equally well to all parties, but in a House which consists increasingly of career politicians whose political futures depend on their compliance, conforming to the party line becomes an essential means of demonstrating loyalty before the armoury of the whips office, especially when set against the prospects of office.

Their numbers vary slightly but, at any one time, there may be as many as 115 MPs and peers on the government's payroll as Ministers, Parliamentary Secretaries or in the Whips Office, together with 30 or so unpaid, Parliamentary Private Secretaries, while a further 113 MPs are effectively appointed by the PM to Parliamentary Select Committees. Like the grand old Duke of York's men, they march and counter march as commanded, while, if doubts should arise as to their orders, there are always the reserves to be mustered, those ambitious back benchers anxious for promotion and willing to plug any gaps in the line of power. For long service and good conduct there is always the prospect of a seat in the Lords. Once, there was a random element to the hereditary system. There is no random element now. New Labour aspirants don't get into the Upper House unless they support the leader, and the executive has no intention whatsoever of agreeing to an elected second chamber, as it should be, preferring to retain it as a quango.

Exactly how many quangos currently exist is difficult to establish. They come and go with the political tide. One thing, however, is certain: potentially, they provide a powerful extension of executive power. In the name of the Crown, the Prime Minister currently appoints the Chairmen and Members of some 340 ecclesiastical and public bodies, ranging from the Archbishops of Canterbury and York, 32 diocesan bishops, and 'two Royal Peculiars', to members of the Board of Customs and Excise, the Board of Inland Revenue, the Head of the Home Civil Service, the Registrar General, the Lord Chief Justice, the Master of the Rolls, and the Lords of Appeal.

This is not all. In addition, the Prime Minister has in his gift the appointment of, amongst others, members of the Honours Scrutiny Committee, the Security Commission, the Committee of Standards in Public Life, and the Surveillance Commissioners, whilst he is expected to be consulted on the appointment of the Chair of a further 70 public bodies, ranging from the BBC, British Nuclear Fuels and the Environment Agency, to the Film Services Authority and the Food Standards Agency. Perhaps most important of all, he appoints our Commissioner in Brussels without the House of Commons even being asked to give its opinion, and, since MEPs are on a party list, the electors only vote for party nominees, and the PM has great influence on who goes to the top of that pecking order.

In short, No. 10 exploits the cat's cradle of patronage to secure the leadership principle of which Blair was to say, 'For a political leader "doing the right thing" in reality is only ever "doing what I think is the right thing".' A chilling statement, the authoritarian undertones of the remark reveals as much about the leadership as it does about the democratic deficit that continues to disfigure the constitution. The danger is that, all too often, the danger goes unrecognized, the more so when, as agents of capital, large sections of the media are party to the process.

Traditionally there were three legs to the constitution, now there is a fourth: the media. Of course, the establishment has always feared a truly free press. An informed public, capable of asking difficult questions about the nature of power, is the last thing they want. Attempts to victimize or censor critical writers and publishers have been at the heart of the constitutional struggle since Milton wrote the *Areopagitica*, and the great jurist Blackstone warned that, 'The liberty of the press is the palladium of all civil, political and religious rights of an Englishman.' Like much else, such rights have been hard won. The question is: how free is the media today?

Persecution and censorship no longer apply, having been replaced by altogether more subtle methods. The dumbing-down of much of the media, to the point where fact and fiction become blurred, smacks of Orwell. While *1984* (1949) remains a dystopian vision, however, the reality is that no political party can afford to spurn the favours of the radio, press and TV. Where it was once the practice to tune the pulpit, today the imperative is to tune the media or, conversely, for the media to fine tune politics. Indeed, the one cannot be divorced from the other. It is a tacit compact in which sections of the media trade their coverage in return for commercial favours. The deal is never explicit; it exists, nonetheless, and the hierarchs of New Labour were quick to grasp that reality. They imposed a rigid, centralized control of the government's information machine in order, amongst other things, to target good days in which 'to bury bad news'.

Currently more than a thousand press and public relations specialists, together with a further 300 press officers in the Central Office of Information, are on the Whitehall pay roll. For those journalists who accept the regime, and who connive at their own manipulation, there is always the promise of 'an exclusive', or an 'off-record briefing' by a minister. Those who do not collude put their careers at risk. Of course, the Parliamentary lobby has always been subject to political pressures – Harold Wilson tried to exclude some journalists from his informal briefings for being critical of his policies – but never more so than today. In fact, there is evidence that the US practice of isolating journalists has been attempted in the UK, Alistair Campbell once going so far as to try to have an editor of the *Independent* sacked for opposing New Labour's policy on Europe.

Altogether more ominously, there are widespread suspicions about the deals being done behind closed doors between media power-brokers and Government, reflected in the story that the Prime Minister struck a deal with Rupert Murdoch to hold a referendum on the EU constitution in order to win News International's support for New Labour. True or not, it is incontestable that Blair backed a communications bill that loosened foreign media ownership and allowed a major newspaper publisher to own a broadcast TV station, as well as a provision its critics called 'the Murdoch clause' because it appeared to apply mainly to News Corporation. Not that the condition is peculiar to New Labour, or that Murdoch is by any means the only media privateer imposing his diktat on the empire he controls, with all the influence that this implies.

Individually each element in this construct of power – of political collusion and the fine tuning of the media – is a cause for grave concern. Collectively, it represents a calculated effort to dumb down the public by marketing politics like some homogenized product off the supermarket shelves, of selling the sizzle rather than the substance of politics. Again, the irony is inescapable. For all the talk of open government and freedom of information, information has never been so tightly controlled.

Yet it may be that people are not quite so naive, not quite so gullible as the spin-meisters and their masters like to suppose. It may be that, as Seattle and Genoa, and the anti-war movement proved, there are a growing number of people who have seen through the charade that passes for a free press, who question the continuum of power, and its agenda. Indeed, the rapid expansion of the Internet, allied to an emergent republic of Bloggers, presents a direct challenge to the established media, a situation in which an increasing number of Citizen Journalists now threaten the imperium of Citizen Kane.

If true, this may do something to account for the public's disillusionment with the existing political order. (In the half century to 2005, turn out at general elections fell by 25 per cent.) Or it may be that, as Peter Mandelson has asserted, 'representative democracy is coming to an end'. He is not alone with the thought. It is becoming a political commonplace, the question being, what is to replace the existing model if representative democracy has, indeed, passed its sell-by date? Too often for comfort the response is to play the TINA card, implying that there is no alternative to cosying-up to neo-liberalism, in which case democracy, with all that the word entails, becomes little more than a pawn to the dictates of globally volatile capital. Three decades have passed since Hailsham identified the problem. Seemingly, the condition is progressive. But then, capital has never had any truck with democracy. On the contrary, in all its many guises it has contested power if not since time immemorial, then certainly since property became the touchstone of government.

As with democracy, the word property defies exact definition. While each has mutated, both have continued to share a symbiotic relationship. It was John Locke who captured the essence both of its power and its resilience: 'The great and chief end of men uniting into Commonwealths, and putting themselves under government, is the preservation of their property.' The court philosopher of the Whig grandees of the eighteenth century, oligarchs who made godhead of property. Locke's prescription served their purposes admirably, as it does for their successors. The balance of the property-political equation may have shifted since he wrote, but the underlying structure of power has remained largely unchanged. Indeed, it has been that capacity of latter-day Whigs to adapt to circumstances which has ensured their survival. Never more so than during the twentieth century.

Tawney may have defined the polarities of power – economic and political – but even he would have been astounded by the changes that have occurred since he wrote. Indeed, the past 60 years have marked a tectonic shift in the balance of global power, as I learned during my time as a member of successive Labour governments. As a minister, I assumed that as far as my own department was concerned, our task was to prepare policies and then, subject to Parliament, to apply them. In my frequent trips to Brussels, I learned how naive I had been.

Since its inception, I always suspected that the Common Market was little more than a capitalist club. This said, and ironic as it might seem, Ted Heath and I shared much in common as far as the European project was concerned. We knew each other for 55 years, and whenever we talked over the subject, Ted would say, 'Look, Tony, Europe slaughtered millions of men in two world wars. We can't let that happen again.' And I agreed, as I did at one time with his argument that Europe could well serve as a counterweight to the burgeoning power of the multinationals, many of whose budgets are larger than those of nation states. In fact, shortly after being appointed Postmaster General, in 1964, I wrote in my diary:

> I was always against the Common Market but the reality of our isolation is being borne in on me all the time. This country is so decrepit and hidebound that only activities in a wider sphere can help escape the myths which surround our politics ... As British economic policy had failed, I thought that Europe might provide the basis for securing some democratic controls over the new, multi-national, mega corporations that were emerging.

How wrong I was. I had still to learn the full extent of my misconception. In 1974, as Industry Secretary, I became a Member of the Council of Ministers, possibly the most interesting experience in my political life. In the next four years, I was to have an insight into the arcane workings of the new European establishment, of the conclave of bureaucrats who set the agenda, and determined the policies of the Market – all behind closed doors. And the more I learned, the more I realized that whatever notion I had of democracy was being overridden by people who had no interest whatsoever in the principle. They were people who, while paying lip service to the ideal, made a charade of it in practice. Seemingly the entire bureaucratic edifice was constructed simply to perpetuate itself, a cat's cradle of power that regarded Parliaments as little more than medieval advisory assemblies, and one which denied Ministers the right to table documents, this being the prerogative of unelected Commissioners who determined the agendas. In short, it was and remains a bureaucracy in which substantive decisions are taken in secret, no one being allowed to hear the debates.

Indeed, it was this, the secrecy surrounding our discussions which, during my Presidency of the Council of Ministers, prompted me to write to my fellow Ministers saying that as we were responsible for making the laws, then we should do so in public. Although I regarded it as a comparatively modest proposal, I was nearly strangled for my troubles. It was only behind the closed doors in Brussels that the real power was exercised. It was here that the real deals were done. And always and everywhere in the interstices of power, there were the lobbyists. Once I believed that the EEC would help to contain their influence. Once again, I was wrong, for the multinationals were quick to exploit Brussels as a means of by-passing and defeating the policies of nation states. Of course, lobbying has always been a feature of government, but it is American practices that have transformed it into the dark art that we know today. An old friend of mine, Jack Gilligan, one time the Democratic Governor of Ohio, used to say, 'You will never get democracy in America as long as big business buys both parties – and gets the pay off whoever wins.' And in these winner-takes-all political stakes, some 35,000 lobbyists now spend more than $5billion a year trying to influence the votes of members of Congress.

So far, the European Union has retained at least a semblance of resistance to 'the big payola'. Nonetheless, the danger remains, which is one reason why, in 1988, I tabled my European Communities (Amendment) Bill calling for 'the return of full and unfettered powers to the United Kingdom over all legislation enacted by the European Communities', with the critical proviso that all members of the Community should continue to work closely with one another. If this was not enough to lay the charge that I was, constitutionally, anti-European, I then worked for five years drafting my Commonwealth of Europe Bill which argued, forcibly, that it was essential for the UK to cooperate closely in the European project, while pointing out that the existing structure of the Community overrode the domestic laws of member states. It further argued that economic union 'would undermine still further the democratic accountability of those with power to those over whom that power would be exercised'.

I used to think that Tony Blair was prepared to sacrifice democracy in Britain as the price one has to pay for what's called 'greater influence in Europe'. By contrast, I now believe that the European super-state is part of the counter revolution against the democratic advances that have been made in Britain, and throughout Europe. Moreover, managed as it is by a European Central Bank that is accountable only to itself, the Euro is an integral part of this transfer of power from the polling station to the market place, from the ballot box to the wallet.

Of course, capitalism never took kindly to the social democratic revolution of the post-war years, and it was Reagan and Thatcher who led the counter revolution. They realized that it was not the military threat of communism that would destroy their privileges, social and economic, but democracy. It was this realization that led to Reagan's attack on the New Deal, and to Thatcher's privatization of large swathes of the economy. In fact, the return of the Tories in 1979 marked an anniversary of sorts, the centenary of Joe Chamberlain's Mayoralty of Birmingham, and the programme of social reforms he launched – among them the public acquisition of such utilities as gas and electricity and transport. It was these municipal purchases that led to Birmingham becoming known as 'the best-governed city in the world'.

Albeit embryonic, Chamberlain's municipal initiative was to provide a model for public sector growth after 1945 – a conscious effort to establish public control over, and the accountability of, Britain's core enterprises and industries: water, electricity, gas; steel, coal, and the railways. For 30 years, under successive Labour and Conservative governments the model survived, only to be dismembered by the New Tories. Hell-bent on re-empowering capitalism, the entire project was anathema as far as the Thatcher administrations were concerned. Disciples of laissez faire, they set about demolishing the entire enterprise piecemeal, returning power to where they believed it belonged: in the free market. Blair and New Labour have continued to celebrate its primacy.

Nothing, it seems, now escapes the creeping privatization of key elements of what remains of the public services, more especially the National Health Service and education. However disguised, the outcome is as damaging as it is insidious. It conceals the profit motive that is driving such 'reforms'. While the market has always been a potent myth, the fact is that it has never been free. On the contrary, it substitutes profit for true competition which leads, progressively, to the concentration of power in mega companies concerned solely with maximizing their returns, and careless of public interest. Significantly, Adam Smith, author of the *Wealth of Nations*, and prophet of today's free marketeers, was quick to recognize that civil government was, 'in reality instituted for the defence ... of those who have property against those who have none'. He was to excoriate a system under which, 'It is the industry which is carried on for the benefit of the rich and powerful, that is principally encouraged, that which is carried on for the poor and the indigent is, too often, either neglected or oppressed.'

Careless of the proviso, it was a formula which the free marketeers of the nineteenth century embraced wholeheartedly, invoking the credo of Richard Cobden that, 'A law which prevents free trade is a law which interferes with Divine Providence'. God may have been dispensed with ... but mammon is alive and well, and living in the theology of globalization. The evidence is indisputable, and there for all to see:

- half of the world's 2.85 billion workers are now existing on less than the $2-a-day poverty line;
- the income of the richest fifth of the world's population is now 74 times that of the poorest fifth;
- 82 per cent of the world's income is now enjoyed by the richest 20 per cent, while 1.4 per cent of the world's income is enjoyed by the poorest 20 per cent;
- 417 billionaires now control as much wealth as the poorest 50 nation states;
- according to the UN Development Agency, 'less that 4 per cent of the personal wealth of the 225 richest people would suffice to offer all the poor of the world access to elementary medical and educational amenities as well as adequate nutrition'.

As the Agency was quick to note, however, 'such a relatively minor redistribution of basic necessities is unlikely to occur, not in the foreseeable future at any rate'. The underlying thrust of their conclusion is clear: on the one hand, that the divide between rich and poor is a direct product of the market (in Britain, the Office for National Statistics revealed in 2005 that the wealthiest 1 per cent of the population had doubled their wealth to £797 billion in the previous six years, while the wealth of the bottom 50 per cent fell from 10 per cent to 5 per cent over the same period); on the other, that while Locke's latter-day acolytes continue to pay lip service to the principle, civil society remains at a discount.

Globally, governance, with all that entails as far as democracy and civil liberties are concerned, remains the preserve of property, while that triad of power, the World Bank, the International Monetary Fund, and the World Trade Organization, provide a patina of legitimacy for the operations of the market. Unelected and accountable only to themselves, they set the rules of a game in which market fundamentalism is championed above all other views, a closed circuit of power that determines the economic agenda, and adapts its rhetoric in order to retain its hegemony.

Except for the market's reach, this is nothing new, rather it is the old, old story of the subordination of political to economic power. While not a conscious conspiracy, it is nonetheless resilient. Where once the market's boundaries were confined largely, though never entirely, to the nation state, the past couple of centuries have changed all that. If the Manchester school of the mid nineteenth century extolled free trade, then its successors in the past half century have idolatrized it, as a secular deity which, following the fall of the Berlin Wall, led Francis Fukuyama to declare that liberal democracy, dependent on the free market, constituted the 'end point of mankind's ideological evolution'. Careless of the fact that there is nothing more ideological than declaring the demise of ideology, the hubris remains.

Individually, the challenges implicit in the interlocking rings of power – economic and political, national and global – are formidable. Collectively, they pose a very real threat to democratic governance and to civil liberty. Since the medieval theologian, Wycliffe, declared that 'our liberties are usurped by manquelers such as God hath condemned', and the Commonwealth radical, Thomas Rainborough, asserted that 'the poorest He in England has a right to live as the greatest He', successive generations have campaigned to curb 'the impudence of power'. They have done so in pursuit of what Tom Paine declared were the Rights of Man. The tides of history have marked the ebb and flow of their aspirations. Nonetheless, the vision remains, the danger being the electorates' growing disenchantment with the political process, a product of the attack on democracy that is at the heart of the process itself.

So much is easily said, the question being, what steps can be taken to reverse the situation? In the UK context, and in this the UK is not alone, there is an urgent need to re-establish the public's confidence in the political process. All too often, the temptation is for people to contract out, convinced either of their capacity to 'go it alone' or, conversely, their inability to influence affairs. Both are corrupting illusions, the more so when manipulated by the media. Indeed, the compulsion to believe in something we want to be true, rather than seeing reality for what it is, can be breathtaking – a form of induced somnambulism.

But again, what can be done if we are not to sleep walk into the future? As I see it, the first step to understanding is to ask three key questions: What is going on? Why is it going on? What can be done about it? If you can answer the first question, you are well on the way to finding out why, and then being able to do something about it. And it is here that the media and education play a vital role. As to the former, politics has been trivialized to the point where the media 'presents a largely imaginary view of life as a celebrity soap opera', this from a 2006 report commissioned by the governors of the BBC. As to the latter, the role played by education has always been contentious. An educated public is the last thing that the establishment wants, which is why the idea of comprehensives, where everyone has access to a full range of knowledge, was seen as a revolutionary doctrine that had to be reversed.

Of course, it may not be entirely coincidental that the 2006 Education Bill, which was drafted to meet this objective, dovetailed with the growing concentration of power in the hands of central at the expense of local government. The conjunction is significant, forming, as it does, one element in the trend towards the consolidation of power not only at national but also at European Union and global levels. And all this at the expense of grass-roots participation in the democratic process.

Indeed, the erosion of local autonomy saps at the very essence of civil society. It is all very well to mock the notion of Power to the People, but that is where ultimate power should reside. Instead of which, instead of devolving power, it is now in the gift of central government. This may go some way in accounting for the low turnout at local elections, as people come to realize how local government has been de-gutted.

This is not to idealize the past. Far from it. There was a time, however, and not so distantly, when local authorities determined their own agendas, and controlled their own budgets; when they built houses, ran schools, and managed the thousand-and-one services that are at the core of local communities. The system may not have been flawless, but it located power where it belonged: locally. No longer. For all the passage of innumerable reorganization schemes, or more insidiously, because of them, local government's powers have been progressively usurped by Westminster, Whitehall and Brussels – all in the name of modernization. If trust is to be restored in the political process, it is imperative that the trend is reversed, that power is restored to local authorities in order to re-engage people in the management of their own affairs.

But then, power is a seductive thing, jealously cosseted by its brokers. Whether Lord Acton was right when he declared that power tends to corrupt, and that absolute power tends to corrupt absolutely remains open to debate. One thing, however, is certain: the greater the concentration of power, the more it is open to abuse. Historically, this has always been the case, and the power-brokers of the so-called Westminster Village are no exception to the rule. Not that piecemeal tinkering with the existing order will rectify the situation. If the cynicism that currently bedevils politics – and it may not be altogether coincidental that the so-called 'democratic deficit' has spawned a new corruption in place of the old – then nothing less than root-and-branch reform of the system will suffice.

More than three centuries have passed since the passage of the Bill of Rights of 1688, the prompt for my Commonwealth of Britain Bill calling for the establishment of 'a democratic, federal and secular Commonwealth of England, Scotland and Wales dedicated to the welfare of all its citizens'. It was conjoined with an updated Charter of Rights: 'All citizens of Britain shall be entitled to enjoy, and campaign for, universal democratic and enforceable rights ... enshrined in law, adhered to in practice and respected by society, as a precondition of self-government and the achievement of full political, social and economic emancipation within a civilized society.'

The one complemented the other, calling, as they did, for the abolition of the constitutional rights of the Crown; for an elected

President, and a Commonwealth Parliament made up of a House of Commons and a House of the People; for Parliament to have powers over governments, including the work of ministers at the United Nations and in Brussels; for the establishment of national Parliaments for England, Scotland and Wales; for the disestablishment of the Church of England, and the entrenchment of religious freedom; and for local authorities to acquire general powers, subject to statute.

A radical agenda? Certainly. But then the crisis of confidence undermining civil society demands nothing less. And if there is a need to curb the 'impudence of power' at national level, the same is equally true of Britain's relationship with the EU, where national sovereignty has been subordinated to the power-brokers of Brussels. Not that this is to question the need for close co-operation between the existing, European nation states. Rather the reverse, which is why, in the 1990s, I tabled a Bill calling for the creation of a wide Commonwealth of Europe to 'lay the foundation for an ever-closer association of the people of Europe ... based on the mutual respect for the fully self-governing status' of all the signatories.

All of which has to be set in a global context where there is mounting evidence that the imperium of the market is not invulnerable. Mrs Thatcher may have declared that, 'There is no alternative' but she was wrong. Cracks are already beginning to appear in the carapace of power: in the United States, where a growing number of questions are being asked about the nature of the neocons' project, and its associated pursuit of 'full-spectrum dominance'; and in China and India and Brazil, where powerful new players in the global game may, in the none-too-distant future, challenge US hegemony; and in the growing appreciation of how fragile is our eco-sphere, and the resulting challenge to the fiction that, 'The market rules, OK?'

Even that prophet of neo-liberalism, Francis Fukuyama, has taken to rewriting 'the end of history' as a result of the seismic shifts that shadow the future: the danger of global warming and the consequent degradation of the environment; the destabilization of the Middle East (after all, Armageddon is a place in Israel); the spectre of global terrorism, and the fear that this induces; the crisis racking sub-Saharan Africa; and the pernicious divide between those who create wealth and those who control it.

If true, if the growing evidence of destabilization is well found, then it is imperative to empower the United Nations if there is to be any hope of creating a stable, international order. Eighty years have passed since the League of Nations collapsed, discredited in part as a result of the US government's refusal to take any part in its proceedings for all that the League was in large part brainchild of President Woodrow Wilson. Once again, due in part to US obstructiveness, there are signs that history is repeating itself. It must not be allowed to happen. For all its shortcomings, the need is to realize the goals set out in the organization's founding charter: 'First, to maintain international peace and security; second, to develop friendly relations among nations based on respect for the principles of the equal rights and self-determination of peoples; third, to achieve international co-operation of an economic, social, cultural and humanitarian character.'

It is easy enough to dismiss such sentiments as the glib response of a generation bloodied in two world wars. They continue to represent admirable objectives, nonetheless, the obstacle being the current nature of global power. If we look at the world today, where power is now international, two things become clear: on the one hand, that national governments elected with democratic objectives are still at the mercy of global forces over which they have little, if any control; on the other, that the struggles that nation states have waged to secure a measure of democracy now have to be re-fought at international level to secure for the United Nations the authority to control, on behalf of the people, those forces that are currently free of such controls – multinational corporations, and the instruments they have created.

No question, they represent a formidable combination of power. And no question, either, that if the UN's original objectives are to be realized then it must have the power necessary to enforce international law against even the most powerful superpower; the power necessary to enforce international standards on multinational corporations, which are otherwise free to exploit weak countries on behalf of the rich; the power necessary to elect and hold accountable the shadow world government that is wholly undemocratic – notably the World Trade Organization, the World Bank, and the International Monetary Fund – to ensure that it is subject to global, democratic control.

An impossible dream? Not so. Whenever I am asked about the prospects for the future I say two things: on the one hand, that my grandchildren's generation are the first in history with the capacity to destroy the human race; on the other, that it has the know-how and technology to solve all the problems we face as the human race. And it is the latter we must cleave to. We must discount pessimism, and assert confidence in our capacity to build a more equitable future, not least by placing the past in context, and remembering what has already been achieved.

Little more than a century has passed since the idea of achieving universal suffrage and votes for women, of securing legitimate status for trade unions, and creating a welfare state had all seemed inconceivable, the stuff of dreams. Indeed, the Labour Party itself emerged from an amalgam of single-issue groups. The Chartists were a single-issue group. The trade unions were a single-issue group. The suffragettes were a single-issue group. Whilst each worked to their own agenda, nonetheless they combined to mobilize the democratic process, and to provide a link between the state and the working class which, in turn, produced the welfare state. It wasn't socialism but, by God, it was the best thing we ever had.

Of course, the ultimate reality is that you can't impose democracy. Either people fight for it, or it doesn't happen. These days we hear a great deal about the corruption of power, but little about the corruption of powerlessness. Yet powerlessness is a corrosive force that demands, in its turn, an equally powerful political response. Seventy years have passed since F. D. Roosevelt declared that 'The only thing we have to fear is fear itself.' The condition is not new. Fear has always been an agent of power. Hitler was by no means the first, and certainly won't be the last, despot to exploit a mood of paranoia to establish his *Führerprincip* ('Unrestricted authority downwards, unrestricted responsibility upwards'), whilst raging at that 'monstrosity of filth and fire' – democracy. And yet it was democracy that prevailed, as it has so often. It is the lesson of history that I never forget.

When the House of Commons caught fire and burned in 1834, Londoners stood across the Thames and cheered. This has always stuck in my mind as a warning of what could happen again if Parliament ceased to represent the people. Then, of course, the Commons did not represent the people. Even the Great Reform Bill of that year gave the vote to fewer than one in ten of the male adult population. It was to take a further 96 years before universal franchise was achieved. I love the Commons, which is not altogether surprising. After all, five members of my family in four generations in three centuries have worked there, and I certainly don't want to see Parliament catch fire again, still less to see people cheering at the spectacle.

An unlikely prospect? Perhaps, but then I am prompted by the memory of what it has taken to achieve what we have, of how many died in the long and often bloody contest to secure a measure of democracy, and of how the past 30 years have revealed, once again, how vulnerable the 'password primeval, democracy', really is.

Chapter 9

Globalization, Exclusion and the Future of Democracy

Tom Hickey

Is the struggle for the democratization of the nation finally over? Is it over not because the task has been achieved but because it has been rendered impossible by the dual effect of repressive political manipulation at home, and the undermining of national autonomy and institutional power by globalization? If so, to what terrain has the struggle migrated? Is there a new democratic ambition that can only be fostered beyond the limits of the nation state? These are questions that express both an anxiety and a yearning. When, in disappointment at the results of the Reform Act of 1832, large sections of the English population reflected sceptically on what use Parliament was for them, a doubt was expressed in that scepticism that has echoed in a cyclical fashion through subsequent generations. We can hear these echoes again today.

How could it be otherwise? Subjects in a state whose government took its population to war on a false prospectus, the majority of the British electorate today has good grounds for contemporary doubt. On 31 October 2006, four years after the Blair/Brown Government embarked on its Iraqi adventure at the behest of its ally in Washington, and with over 650,000 Iraqi deaths as a result of a war that was illegal under the terms of international law, the majority of the British electorate's parliamentary representatives in the Commons (including all but 12 New Labour MPs) rejected a motion for an inquiry into the conduct of that war. The governing party's MPs voted to reject the motion, let us be clear, despite their certain knowledge that the majority of the electorate believes the invasion to have been a mistake, and that it knows that it was lied to by its Government, and that it wants the troops brought home. The New Labour MPs voted against an inquiry despite the knowledge that an even larger majority of their Party's members and supporters is of the same opinion. Who in Parliament then represents this majority view that the failed imperial adventure should be ended, and the troops brought home? How is it possible that this majority cannot exercise its will in this 'democracy'?

If that is the most immediate and obvious malaise afflicting parliamentary democracy at this moment, it is not alone in its corrosive effect. Those acquainted with British politics over the last decade or more will know that the majority of the electorate also favours the re-nationalization of the rail network and the operating companies. This is a majority that is equally hostile to privatization, and is anxious about the future of the NHS. It believes Britain to be distressingly unequal in the distribution of its national income, and is willing to pay more income tax for health and for education. Yet these views are also rarely if ever represented in mainstream politics. This then the great unacknowledged paradox of the political terrain – that political expression and organization are free, after generations of struggle for the popular franchise under the banner of 'democracy', but that the political system now ensures that the enfranchized majority remains unrepresented.

Moreover, if this paradox was a characteristic of the second half of the twentieth century, it is also, in its continuance into the next, only one challenge to the viability of democracy. It is joined today at the start of the twenty-first century, by new threats to both the latter's prestige and to its operation. These fall under the names of neo-liberalism and globalization.

Democracy, as an anticipation, has traditionally offered hope in presenting itself as the mechanism for the attainment of emancipation and liberty. As an accomplished fact (narrowly understood as universal adult suffrage), and after centuries of democratic struggle, it has now subverted the ambitions that inspired those struggles by becoming the means by which popular dissent and dissatisfaction are neutralized. We are told not to complain because 'you get the government you deserve', and because 'these are your policies, freely voted for'. All opposition to government edicts, sanctioned by Parliament, are condemned as anti-democratic, or dismissed as parochial.

Thus 'democracy' as a slogan is both a snare and an illusion. It now functions moreover as myth. It functions, that is, as a word which acts to silence rather than to encourage opposition, and as a word that is assumed to name the politically good. It is a concept whose content is rarely analysed, and whose current form is treated as natural and beyond question. Its currently dominant form (a representative legislature selected periodically through universal adult suffrage, and subject to an essentially fixed and inherited set of individual rights and property laws) is taken to be universally valid, and legitimately to be imposed on others – by force of arms, if necessary. None of these treatments of it are remotely adequate, as the selective moments of the struggle for democracy's realization addressed in this volume have demonstrated. Democracy does not always produce good consequences in its existing institutional form or in others; it is not natural but rather the result of human reflection and action; and its dominant contemporary form is not historically pre-eminent or remotely adequate to its purpose. We have seen how, in English history, the struggle for democracy has always been the struggle of the people, variously embodied in the movements of their time, to wrest power from the minority who wished jealously to cleave that power to themselves. We have also seen how that struggle was never disconnected from issues of justice and equality but was rather provoked always by precisely those concerns.

Today then, democracy faces a twin crisis of legitimacy – a domestic crisis and an international challenge. It appears to be assaulted from within and from without. Domestically, popular aspirations and sentiment are systematically discounted by the ubiquitous, market-friendly, neo-liberal policies advanced and enacted by Tory and New Labour parties alike. Secure in the knowledge that they cannot face any serious threat of being outmanoeuvred on the left, both of the main parties in the UK now compete to win the confidence only of the business sector and of press barons. They contest elections primarily through the influence of those media barons, and through the construction of increasingly expensive popular images of their leaders as men or women who are caring, who are 'prudent', and who can be trusted. This disdain shown to them drives some of the electorate out of the formal political process altogether, and into a variety of movements that express exasperation at the cynicism and self-serving nature of electoral politics. More typically, however, it drives many to the abandonment of any and all political engagement, and into apathetic resignation.

Domestic disillusionment is then exacerbated by a rhetoric of exclusion which the Blair/Brown governments have raised to a high art, and to which they became habituated as a reflex, pre-emptive strike against criticism from the left. This is a process of scape-goating and victimization that is designed to appeal to aspects of popular prejudice, is couched in the terms of reactionary populism, and which marginalizes distinct segments of the population, and attempts to terrorize the victims and their sympathizers into silence. Most obvious in this respect is the demonization of Islam, an orchestrated campaign launched in 2006 by Jack Straw with an attack on the wearing of the veil, and then gradually signed up to (in drip-feed fashion) by 12 government ministers, and quickly followed by the suggestion that tutors in universities should spy on their 'asian-looking students'. None of this as government policy, the electorate was assured, but in the interests of opening debate. Not a debate with Muslims, or with veil wearers, of course, many of whom were thereby driven further out beyond the boundaries of legitimate expression and towards the dangers of communal self-reference and inward-looking self-defence.

This was the second step of a policy that began with the government's invention of the distinction between 'good' and 'bad' Muslims, initially colluded in by some leaders of British Muslims. By 'bad Muslims' was meant, in part, terrorists and fundamentalists, thus linking Islam and terrorism in the public eye. It also meant

political and religious 'radicals', i.e. those who did not intend pas-
sively to accept the government's foreign policy whether in Iraq, in
Afghanistan or in Lebanon and Palestine, and those opposed to a
secular political system. The desperation of this diversionary tactic
was evident as the occupation of Iraq rapidly unravelled into bloody
chaos. Its effects in terms of inter-communal hostility and violence,
verbal and physical, against British Muslims was no less evident, and
no less predictable. Once some of the consequences in terms of
alienation became clear, even government ministers (notably Home
Secretary, John Reid) drew back. Radicalism and terrorism were
belatedly discovered not to be the same thing.

This process, used to marginalize and exclude all radical criticism
of foreign policy, was not new. Its domestic precedents are
numerous. The Blair/Brown distinction between 'hard-working
families' and the indigent constituted the reinvention of the nineteenth-century distinction between the 'deserving' and the 'unde-
serving' poor. Its political benefit was to consign those critical of
government policy over poverty and inequality into a difficult corner where they could be represented as defenders of 'welfare
scroungers', and thus silenced. That this is a rhetorical strategy
entirely lacking in honesty, honour and integrity, and will be viewed
as such by posterity, seems not to concern its practitioners or its
authors. It is a strategy that has been employed by Home Office
ministers in relation to 'hoodies', anti-social behaviour, and the
visible and voluble young, and was deployed in defence of anti-social
behaviour orders (the ASBO system).

If the sharpest example of marginalization can be seen in the
government's encouragement of Islamaphobia, however, its most
insidious example can be found in the introduction of ID cards. The
self-delusory justification for this enormous expense as a count-
terrorism measure is found convincing by few of the electorate – the
London bombers would, after all, have carried their ID cards with
them as they consigned themselves and others to death and mutilation. Behind the empty rhetoric of national security lies the
advantage of turning nurses and doctors and teachers and librarians
and municipal clerks into unpaid extensions of the immigration

service, checking on the 'entitlement' of all who seek to use a service. Only those with a card will be judged to have contributed to the provision of the services they now claim, and will be reported if they attempt to claim without that authorizing card. The consequence will be tens of thousands without housing advice, without dental and medical care, without education for their children, without trade union rights, and without legal protection.

Let us reflect on what such a notion of 'entitlement' implies. This is about belonging; it is about identity in the sense of the definition of 'us' – who 'we' are, as opposed to 'them'. Always a slippery and potentially unsettling idea for us as individuals (given our varied lineages, known and unknown), this notion of identity and belonging is plagued by intractable difficulties at the level of communities and of nations. Those difficulties are now short-circuited. Rightful belonging is now to be defined by the possession of the card, and the card will guarantee that the bearer meets the qualifications, and can legitimately claim her entitlements. Our identities, and our relations with others, will henceforth be fixed, as will the identity of that multi-nation called Britain.

That to which such a proposal remains wilfully blind is the transformed nature of the borders that are today the political divisions both of regional and global commercial and productive activity, and of citizenship. It is not simply that these borders are increasingly becoming defensive fortifications (such as the filmic installations and photographs of Christopher Stewart have recently interrogated, capturing the paranoia and insecurity of a Britain and a world in which civil liberties are rapidly eroded by surveillance and intrusion), they have become key elements in the political economy of productive competition. Increasingly, the economic viability of major sectors of metropolitan economies are becoming dependent on the 'export-processing zones' serviced by a reserve army of labour that is kept outside those economies, and thus deprived of the welfare, health and educational benefits available to those who 'belong'. This labour is, however, no less integral to the economic activity that makes those benefits possible. These borders, moreover, are not just the barbed curtains of exclusion on the frontiers. As

French philosopher, Etienne Balibar, has noted, they are borders that have been imported into the heart of the metropolis. They are the invisible borders which separate those who are 'entitled' and those who are marginal inside the territory of the national or multinational state. They surround the black economies of economically advanced states; they ring the sweatshops of Chicago, Paris, Naples, Manchester and London; they delimit and they disfigure the lives of those who inhabit the territory but who do not have paper or card to legitimize their location, and to secure their identities.

This is the constitution (in the sense of a 'making') of a population that is constituted *as* inferior; it is inferior in rights and is inferior in dignity, and is subjected to violent security control that exists permanently at these borders of Europe. These migrants exist *permanently* at the borders of Europe but are actually *inside* Europe because the borders are now within those cities in which the identity cards of the future will have to be carried. This is not a population that is being excluded by the new controls. It is rather a population that, in the very illegality of its status, is being *included* via criminalization: the *sans papiers* of Paris or Marseille, and elsewhere in France; the *clandestinazione* of Italy, and the tens of thousands of people existing 'on the borders' but *within* our country – such as the Chinese cockle-pickers of Morecambe Bay.

The disadvantage to those who can claim 'entitlement' is of a different kind and a different order. For them, the registered and recognized citizens, the disadvantage is, on the one hand, one of false ownership. They believe themselves to be the proprietors of their identity, to possess their entitlements and their defining characteristics, whereas these have been ascribed to them by fiat. They have been told with whom it is that they can identify. The exercise profoundly compromises democracy. The creation of internal borders between the included and the excluded imprison the former as much as they terrorize the latter: they feel themselves to be accepted and established and able to participate only because of the border within which they have been placed. They have implicitly accepted the terms of their inclusion – their participation is conditional.

Insuperable, and seemingly natural, borders between people will be imposed on their imaginations. It could be better expressed, perhaps, that the borders will be subjectively *appropriated* by people; the subjects, to whom those borders will be delivered from on high, will be the agents of their own consignment. These will not be *their own* borders or *their own* identities but rather borders and identities chosen by the state. It will seem to us that we actively adopt an identity as the natural inheritors of a culture and a location, whereas what is actually happening is the ascription of an identity to us. In return for colluding in this process, we enjoy the rights to education, to political expression, to assembly, to security, and even to some welfare protection. Moreover, in accepting the card, we are also provided with a sense of national belonging. With that sense of belonging comes its reciprocal – a system of exclusion. If there is inclusion there must also be exclusion, and hence the divisions then between natives and foreigners, between us on the one hand and the stigmatized on the other.

Thus are those that 'belong' turned outwards defensively as a phalanx, resentful and wary of the world, and doubtful about the status and trustworthiness of each other. This is neither a stable nor a comfortable position. It is, however, part of a new 'politics of suspicion' which is being foisted upon us, in which our natural reflex will come to be to distrust those whom we meet. Such a politics is entirely incompatible with the necessary political practices of any self- governing civic community. These must include open debate and forceful argument between opposed and incompatible interests, and between those within each interest group, sector or class who have different definitions of those interests. This is a condition for democracy not in the pursuit of some ideal, rational consensus between incompatible interests, but rather to clarify the terms of the conflict and what is at stake for all sides. Open debate, indeed any civic conversation at all, is rendered impossible by generalized suspicion. The notion of inscribed identities is, in any event, entirely inconsistent with the manner in which real identities are formed. These have never been, and cannot be, a set of fixed allegiances, characteristics and self-representations. As the temporal and historical beings that we are, we have our identities shaped by the circumstances and context into which we emerge but then, as active and self-conscious beings, we progressively shape those identities in response to the challenges and elective affinities which we confront and which we choose. We are in that sense self-fashioning beings. In other words, built into the heart of government ID-card policy is an inconsistency with what human identity must be – a fluid and evolving process, not a static condition.

The contrast then is between a citizenship based on such an ascribed and fixed identity or one that is based on human activity and self-definition. The choice of the former that our government has made is not innocent. Nor is its determination to orchestrate the imposition of a revised identity a new departure for states; it has its precedents. To discover the intellectual origins of this idea of ascribed identity one needs to return to the beginnings of the last century, and to the 1920s and 1930s in Germany. Here, the renowned jurist and social theorist, Karl Schmidt, claimed that identity was something that was always and completely ascribed by the state and the political order, and that politics was actually nothing more than adjusting the relationships between such identities. Democracy, moreover, for Schmidt, was stipulated as referring to nothing more than the representation of unity between the people (captured and described by such ascribed identities), on the one hand, and their rulers, on the other. Schmidt celebrated this fact, and further observed that, as long as you had the maximum amount of homogenization within a society, the closer can the state approximate to democracy so defined. In other words, only if you exclude those who are not like you can you have an effective democracy.

Now, it is deeply inconvenient for Mr Blunkett and Mr Clarke and Dr Reid that they do not know (at least I hope that they do not know) the lineage from which the ideas that subtend their ID-card project emerge, and the principles on which those ideas and the project are based. They would of course have no sympathy with Karl Schmidt's notion of politics, or with his Nazism. What they would think (and admit to) about his idea of democracy might be a different matter. Thankfully, Schmidt is wrong both about identity and about democracy, and by extension (if unwittingly) so are Blunkett and Clarke and Reid.

Identities are not formed by inscription; nor are they delivered to us from on high. Identities are forged from what people actually do, by the circumstances in which they strive for life and fulfilment, and by the associations that they are forced to build simply in order to survive. Identities are actively constructed by the solidarities that people grow to feel, and by the cognitive recognition of the common interests they share and the enemy plans they manage to discern. That is what makes identities. Collective identity in that sense is not, therefore, a *given* thing. It is *not* something that *underpins* our capacity to act or to be agents in the world; it is rather the result of past actions and their complex intersection with our present acts, and with the plans and hopes that we hold. Identity then is the *result* of agency, not the other way round.

In history, then, new actions and new agencies lead to new solidarities, and thus to new identifications. The real citizen of Athens, according to Aristotle, was not the passive inscriptively present individual, defined by descent from a family line, and located in a particular geographical location. Aristotle described this as a popular but hasty definition. The true citizen was rather the *active* citizen, the one who was practised in the arts of government and adjudication. So also, for Aristotle, was the polity not defined by reference to geographical boundaries or frontiers but rather by the ambit of the citizens' actions, and by the citizens' aims and their objectives. Who and what we are as subjects, how we imaginatively perceive ourselves, are features constituted at the unstable point of our existences. They emerge at the cusp of our economic circumstances and our economic interests, and at the moments of our recognition of the relationship between these circumstances and interests on the one hand, and our imaginative representation of ourselves to ourselves, and how we see these selves relating to other people.

This is always an unstable ground, both politically and philosophically, but its very instability is a source of strength. It is also what makes the unwitting ambitions of the Home Office's ID-card policy not just otiose but actually impossible to deliver. They can spend vast resources, and our taxes, on the creation of the requisite infrastructure for centralized personal information, and they can attempt to coerce the population into carrying the plastic card. They cannot change the way in which identities are formed as a matter of fact. Neither can they force us to think ourselves other than as we do.

This is not mere philosophical speculation, of only limited relevance to politics or to the question of democracy. In an age when the dominant political rhetoric is about division, entitlement and separation, the incompatibility between rhetoric and reality was palpable in the streets of Edinburgh and in the lanes around Gleneagles when 250,000 people laid siege to the G8 summit in July 2005 in the Make Poverty History protest. They were there to protest at the hunger, debt, disease and underdevelopment that commerce imposes on most of the world's population. The gulf between democracy and 'our democratic system' was evident in the 2,000,000-strong London demonstration against the US invasion of Iraq, and the decision of most of our Parliamentary representatives to ignore it, and to ignore the majority opposition to war that it expressed. In both protests, the complex, fluid and continually reforming identifications of the people were evident. In the greater part, on both occasions, the participants were carriers of British passports but their identification was elsewhere. In the Edinburgh protest, it was with the wretched of the earth. In the London demonstration, it was with those who were about to lose their livelihoods, their homes, their relatives and their lives, and it was with all those of the world's population who, in more attenuated ways, were going to suffer from the construction of a new American Empire. What were the effective if imagined borders that gave these protesters their identities on these occasions?

If governmental tactics challenge the viability of democracy domestically then the policies and the circumstances of the nation's position in today's world seem to many to have buried democracy as a feasible short-term objective. In this respect there are two forces at work: policy choices and treaties freely entered into, on the one hand, and the erosion of the power of nation states to determine their own destinies as a result of objective changes in international economic relations, on the other. If the power of the nation state is being fatally eroded, and if the nation state is the sole site of institutions that can host a contest for power between different constituencies, then the struggle for democracy, for the exercise of the popular will, has been deprived of its battle ground. If life is shaped by distant bureaucrats (and politicians who represent governments rather than peoples or the people) in Strasburg or Brussels or Washington or New York, and over whom voters have no control, then why vote? If parliaments and their elected deputies can only debate technical questions about *policy implementation*, having accepted a Washington Consensus in which there are no radical *policy choices* to be made, why bother to elect the deputies? In such circumstances it will seem to increasing numbers of the electorate that citizenship, and the associated political rights and duties attaching to it, have been evacuated of content. Both the idea of democracy in general, and all of its rituals and practices, will seem like a charade. It will seem that to practise them would be to perform one's own entrapment by a myth.

Here then we have a world in which there has been a conscious and intentional relinquishment of the main elements of *sovereign deliberation* to supranational bodies – to the European Union, to the United Nations, to the World Trade Organization and the International Monetary Fund, and to the International Court of Justice, etc. Here also is a world in which there is, irrespective of such foreign policy choices, the *de facto* erosion of elements of *sovereign effects*. The scope for the exercise of what remains of economic sovereignty is severely limited by processes beyond the control of nation states – the global environmental effects of other states' policies, the demographic effects of uneven development and climate change, and the redistribution of capital flows, and evolving trade patterns. The only role for governments then appears to be prescribed by the 'Anglo-Saxon model': to manage a race to the bottom in terms of wage rates, labour conditions and tax-funded welfare systems in order to maintain employment levels at a tolerable level.

In these conditions, it has been argued, the struggle for democracy has reached its terminus. Democracy is only possible if citizens can, at least potentially, be in control of the political processes and institutions. This requires well-defined institutions with sovereign power, and a delimited citizenship to exercise its political rights in controlling these institutions. Yet neither exists today. Many of the most important decisions that impact on the people's well-being are taken beyond the reach of the political citizen – in global forums, or in corporate boardrooms, or in conference halls of international organizations. At three or four steps removed from the electoral process, or unaffected by it at all, such decisions are 'beyond democratic accountability'.

A distinct yet related reflex of this argument can also be found in a growing scepticism about the substance of citizenship itself. We inhabit territories where many are excluded from formal citizenship, and where territorially located decisions impact across borders. We inhabit polities in which there is an unprecedented concentration of media power, and a rapid decline of mid-twentieth-century public-service broadcasting. This shift in the political economy of communication has enabled the deployment of new communication technologies and the anaesthetizing culture of popular titillation and trivialization in a manner that secures the systematic mis-representation of reality. Facts are distorted; conflicting interest and conflicts are misrepresented and traduced. These developments, taken together with the decline in popular sites and provocations for discussion and debate (the club or pub, the trade union meeting, the political rally, the committed or informative newspaper and the political tract or pamphlet), have progressively dissolved what the German critical theorist Jürgen Habermas has called 'the public sphere'. Without such an arena, it is argued, no source for democratic aspiration exists.

More fundamentally, there has been a progressive erosion of the sense of community, of the idea of a shared project in the nation, and of the nexus of shared values and norms that cemented a population as a group. What is lost is a stable social bond, and hence the possibility of a stable political society. The loss, or at least the erosion, of state autonomy and territorial sovereignty and integrity then further weakens these social bonds and the sense of national identity. In such a world, it is argued, democracy becomes untenable – a people that loses its sense of history and continuity, and its distinctiveness from those excluded from its political rights, can never exercise its democratic voice and potential. It will have lost its reference point; no longer able to identify its collective interest against those outside its embrace, it will no longer have reason to debate policy, or to agonize over hard policy choices. Thus, to the extent that it makes porous the boundaries of the nation and the borders of the nation state, is the process of globalization incompatible with democracy as hitherto understood. According to such a view, the 'democratic deficit' which ought to concern us is not the deficiencies of electoral processes in exercising some representative control over executive decision-making in the European Union but rather the impossibility of electoral processes furthering the democratic ambition at all. It is not that Tony Benn is mistaken in his judgement concerning the European Union's impact on democracy but rather that his remedy constitutes no more than a romantic nostalgia in a world dominated by global financial flows, and by transnational corporate decisions that respond only to global market conditions, and which are beyond the control of governments. There is no possibility, it is argued, of popular sovereignty in a constituency that now supervenes the nation state – and it is that global space that is the relevant constituency today.

It is such considerations that have given rise to the argument for a reconceptualization of citizenship, and for the development of the idea of a 'transnational' or 'global' citizenship. Associated with this ambition is the idea of re-focusing the struggle for democracy in terms of its ambition, and re-positioning the struggle from engagement with domestic processes to the construction of international ones. The project goes under the name of Cosmopolitan Democracy. It is the radical alternative to the conservative reaction to the challenge of globalization. For the later, the appropriate plea is for a return to the nation, to reconnect with the community out of which the nation springs, and thus to recuperate and recover those sovereign powers from which the national community has been alienated. In respect of political movements, this conservative reaction has two distinct and antagonistic wings: that which emphasizes the unifying force of the nation, and that which places its focus on the sub-national communities which the nation once unified, and which consequently is concerned with local interests and local struggles. Against both, Cosmopolitan Democracy offers a vision of the extension of democracy beyond the limits of the nation state, and a mechanism, in various forms, of world government. Is it necessary, is it viable, is it desirable?

Without doubt, the proposal for a new cosmopolitanism arises from the recognition of real changes in the global economy, and of the consequences of these for national sovereignty, and hence for popular sovereignty. The aspiration of this new cosmopolitanism is to discover a means for the renewal of democracy, and to do so in a manner that will enable the development of popular control (or at least influence) in an increasingly globalized world. It is an aspiration to develop a formal political expression (in the sense of political institutions and processes and parties and alliances) for the sentiments that motivate the engagement with activist politics. Its aim is to produce a site for debate and decision-making open to the millions who oppose the new Imperialism, who wish to battle poverty and underdevelopment and inequality, and who demand an urgent address to the problems of impending environmental catastrophe.

As soon as the aim has been expressed, however, the problem of implementation becomes stark. What would the site for this debate be? It could not be the United Nations, given that the UN is no more than an assembly of government representatives. If the democratic process in nation states is compromised by corporate globalization, by the systematic misinformation of the mass media, and by the use of democratic rhetoric for repressive ends, then the representation of that inadequate process internationally will constitute no solution.

Current forms of global representation at second or third hand (deputies voted for in elections, who then select governments, which then appoint global or regional representatives) are part of the problem to be addressed. Yet direct representation seems practically infeasible. What would the constituencies be which would return elected delegates or representatives, and how large would they have to be to prevent an assembly becoming impossibly unwieldy? If one was commencing the blueprint for future world government there could be little reason simply to accept the inheritance of the national divisions that are products of accident and the most invidious of histories. But on what other basis? Even were these problems to be resolved, there is then the question of which institutions or entities there are over which a democratic world polity would be able to exercise its powers. The record of nation states in exercising internal control over the self-interested drives and consequent rapacious behaviours of the corporate sector are hardly signal in their success.

Moreover, it is entirely unclear why national governments would exert their influence to produce this form of enhanced global democratic governance. For them to do so would be a *de facto* admission of their own partial impotence in the face of global trends. It would also be to admit their own inadequacy and culpability in this new democratic deficit, and thereby to consign themselves to marginality if not to irrelevance. But if not governments as the agency for such a transformation, then who or what might pursue such a strategy to a successful conclusion? It is one thing to organize anti-imperialist and anti-war demonstrations of enormous size and sophistication, to weld disparate and sometimes hostile groupings together in such initiatives, and to coordinate such protests across national frontiers and even between continents. It is quite another thing to secure the structural changes consequent on a reform of the mechanisms of governance. Protests can be coordinated; reforms need to be won in an existing arena and to be implemented by an existing executive. If no such arena or compliant executive exists then it is revolution rather than reform that is required. It is for these reasons that the project for a new cosmopolitanism in the form of 'democratic global governance' seems extraordinarily unlikely.

It is arguable, however, that the project's infeasibility may be the least of its problems. There are also the questions of whether it is necessary and desirable. The argument, let us recall, is predicated on

190

the erosion of state autonomy by global forces. The difficulty here is that nation states still retain enormous control, not only of their subjects but also of the behaviour of their citizens overseas, and an enormous interest in the operation of their national corporations overseas. Equally, they are not powerless in influencing the decisions of inward-moving capital. They can attract it through appropriate infrastructural investment, tax breaks, the creation of capital-friendly regimes of industrial relations, and by promises to use the influences of state power on its behalf, regionally and globally. They can exercise control over domestically-located foreign capital, through alterations in fiscal policies and the amendment of corporate reg-ulations. In attempting to understand the relationship between global capital and nation states, we should not be misled by the ubiquitous, self-serving and liberal contemporary rhetoric about this being a one-way street. Nation states are still today the key political sites for profit making and for the deployment of productive and infrastructural resources; and they are the only units that are both materially equipped and morally empowered by international law to exercise force of arms in the protection of those resources.

Is the proposal for democratic global governance as an element of an immediate political agenda desirable? Part of the argument here is that a global 'civil society' needs to be constructed which can form the basis, if not for the election of a world government, then at least for a monitoring of the activities of national governments. What this assumes is that no such civil society yet exists at a global level, and that the existence of a viable and vibrant civil society would, in and of itself, be sufficient to advance the democratic project. In fact, there already exists more than the roots of a global civil society. This takes the form of the various clubs and societies and meetings of the CEOs of the major transnational companies which constitute themselves as a band of brothers, however much engaged they are in mutual competition. Various studies from the first years of this century have demonstrated the self-conscious emergence of these elite groups and their organizations. They constitute, in effect, the recognition of a trans-capitalist interest, and they organize in order to develop the requisite strategic and moral visions to defend those

191

interests, and the consequent policy frameworks that result. They have existed since the end of the Second World War in private form as exemplified by the Mont Pelerin Society and the Bilderberg Conferences; they exist today as conjunctions of such public and private international policy-making groups as the World Economic Forum, the Trilateral Commission, and the World Business Council for Sustainable Development. Part of their latent function is precisely to create not simply a collective will that can pursue their interests but also the collective intellectuals (their policy centres) that can defend and operationalize those wills.

It is not that this civil society is one-sided. Counterposed to this emergence of what could be called (and would once have been called) a transnational ruling class, are the various non-governmental organizations whose project is to contest the worst consequences of global commerce, if not its purposes and existence. These are the defenders of environmental protection, the seekers after sustainable development, and the critics of global poverty. However admirable their purposes and their efforts, neither should be confused with the democratic project. Democratic structures do not exist in which such pressure groups can operate. Theirs is an often heroic endeavour to expose the inhumanity, the barbarism and the myopia of their antagonists, and to secure a level of popular support for their projects sufficient to persuade elements of the corporate sector, in their own self interest, to mend their ways. In such an endeavour, democracy would be at best superfluous, and might even be an encumbrance.

The difficulty for democrats today with all cosmopolitan projects is that by implying the partial irrelevance of local political processes and structures, and by suggesting the growing impotence of national governments, these arguments operate in a manner that tends to disarm and demobilize the people. By suggesting the possibility of a global culture as a substitute for the peculiarities of national identity, it loses sight of the fact that it is from national cultures that notions of fairness and justice emerge, which, when universalized, lead to mass movements for global human rights and material well being. As observed above, these cultural identities are not fixed but they are rooted in the particularities of different national communities. To ignore this fact is to set one's vision apart from history, and is to conflate particularity with parochiality.

If the inadequacies of existing democratic processes challenge us, and the appeals for a new cosmopolitan democracy cannot inspire us, what then may be done? The starting point must be recognition of the great advance made for humanity by the 'alternative globalization movement'. Here is a movement, insistent these days upon that designation, as opposed to 'anti-globalization', which celebrates the growing interconnectedness of the world and the potential thereby inscribed. In the same breath, however, it voices its disdain for those who conclude from this process of globalization that only neo-liberal policies are possible as practical politics. This is a movement that identifies with each and every struggle of local populations, organizes solidarity for them, and publicizes their cause. It is a movement that confronts the global clubs and meetings of the powerful with expressions of popular anger. And it is a movement that has begun the process of constructing a positive agenda through the organization of a series of regional and world Social Forums.

Nevertheless, even this movement, while redolent of grievance and determined agency, and with a universalist attitude of which Enlightenment rationalists would have been proud, has not yet identified how best to operate in relation to the existing levers of power and structures of representation in a manner that might secure lasting political change. One is reminded here of Tony Benn's quip, on retiring from Parliament, that he was leaving the Commons 'in order to spend more time with his politics'. It is in this sense that politics now exists beyond the ranks of those institutions in which it was once framed. The struggle for democracy, and for human betterment, has long ceased to be a project of the Labour Party, and has never been part of the impoverished vision of New Labourism. However vibrant this politics beyond politics may be, it requires an expression within the existing democratic structures in order to draw the interest and involvement of an ever-wider constituency. It is through this process of cross-fertilization that the democratic forces can be advanced, and can exercise their influence in transforming the political structures. Such a project is precisely about transforming these structures beyond recognition, rendering them responsive to popular ambition because under popular control, and not simply transparent and accountable while operated by professional politicians. The problem that exists is to identify the political agency that might cohere such a movement of movements within each nation state.

In the case of Britain, it was once an open question whether the Labour Party could be recaptured for democracy and could recuperate from the effects of the Blair/Brown neo-liberal project. It would be hard today to find many who still consider this question to be open. It is here, perhaps, that the role of trade unions re-emerges. At one stage the orchestrators and power-brokers of the Labour Party's birth, and throughout its history acting as the mordant hand of gradualism and conformity, the unions today find themselves with a pressing responsibility. Their ability to represent and defend their members' interests still suffers from the consequences of the anti-trade union legislation of the 1980s and 1990s. These anti-union laws have been preserved intact by the Blair/Brown governments even as the restructuring of health, welfare, and education provision adversely affected the interests of both providers and users of these services, whether unionized or not. Now must be the moment, one would have thought, for a reconsideration of old loyalties and allegiances. The trade unions, moreover, remain the sole repository of democratic ambition in its substantive sense that have retained the organizational strength and popular support to play such a formative role yet again. They will need, however, to lose those elements of nostalgia that have long been characteristic of British labour politics. As Bertolt Brecht was reported once to have said as a maxim for clear sightedness: 'Don't start from the good old things but the bad new ones.'

Further reading

Introduction

Coates, D. (1975), *The Labour Party and the Struggle for Socialism*, Cambridge: CUP.

Davis, A. J. (1992), *To Build a New Jerusalem: The British Labour Movement from the 1880s to the 1990s*, Michael Joseph.

Eley, G. (2002) *Forging Democracy: the History of the Left in Europe, 1850–2000*, Oxford: OUP.

Elliott, G. (1993), *Labourism and the English Genius: the Strange Death of Labour England?*, Verso.

Foot, P. (2005), *The Vote: How it was Won and How it was Undermined*, London: Penguin.

Hinton, J. (1983), *Labour and Socialism: A History of the British Labour Movement, 1867–1974*, Wheatsheaf, Hassocks.

Manning, B. (1991), *The English People and the English Revolution*, London: Bookmarks.

Meiksens Wood, E. (1995), *Democracy Against Capitalism*, Cambridge: CUP.

Morton, A. L. (1992), *A People's History of England*, London: Lawrence & Wishart.

Rees, J. (2006), *Imperialism and Resistance*, London: Routledge.

Chapter 1

Campbell, J., *Anglo-Saxon England*, BBC.

Dobson, B., *The Revolt of 1381*.

Dobson, B. and John Taylor, *Rymes of Robin Hood*, 2nd Edn.

Christopher Dyer is the current authority on diet and living standards, as on deserted villages.

—— Anglo-Saxon England – collected essays.

Further reading

Fryde, E., *The English Peasantry of the Late Middle Ages*.
—— *The Peasants' Revolt of 1381*, Historical Association pamphlet.
Hilton, R., *The English Peasantry of the Thirteenth Century*.
—— *The Later Medieval English Peasantry*.
—— *Bondmen Made Free*.
Hoskins, W.G. and R.H. Tawney *passim*
Knight, S. (ed.) *Robin Hood*.

Chapter 2

Hill, Christopher (1986), *The World Turned Upside Down*, London, Penguin.
Hughes, Ann (1998), *The Causes of the English Civil War*, Basingstoke.
Mendle, Michael, ed. (2001), *The Putney Debates of 1647*, Cambridge.
Whatmore, Richard (1998), *The Weber Thesis: unproven yet unrefuted*, in *Historical Controversies and Historians*, ed., William Lamont, London.
Woodhouse, A. S. P. (1938), *Puritanism and Liberty*, London: J. M. Dent and Sons.

Chapter 3

Anderson, D. (2006), *Histories of the Hanged: Testimonies from the Mau Mau Rebellion in Kenya*, London: Phoenix.
Blunt, W. Scawen (2007), *Secret History of the English Occupation of Egypt*, (1922), Stroud: Nonsuch Publishing.
Danner, Mark (2006), *The Secret Way to War*, New York: New York Review of Books.
Elkins, C. (2005), *Britain's Gulag: The Brutal End of Empire in Kenya*, London: Pimlico.
Fisk, R. (2006), *The Great War For Civilisation: the Conquest of the Middle East*, London: Harper Perennial.
Harrison, R. (1995), *Gladstone's Imperialism in Egypt*, Greenwood Press, Westport.
Lucas, W. Scott (1991), *Divided We Stand: Britain, the United States and the Suez Crisis*, London: Hodder and Stoughton.
Trocki, C. A. (1999), *Opium, Empire and the Global Political Economy: a Study of the Asian Opium Trade*, London: Routledge.
Wong, J., P. Hannan and D. Twitchett (1998), *Deadly Dreams: Opium,*

Imperialism and the Arrow War (1856–1860) in China, Cambridge: CUP.

Chapter 4

Burns, A. and J. Innes (2003), *Rethinking the Age of Reform: Britain 1780–1850*, Cambridge: CUP.

Foot, P. (2005), *The Vote: How it was Won and How it was Undermined*, London: Penguin.

Pearce, E. (2003), *Reform: The Fight for the 1832 Reform Act*, London: Pimlico.

Roberts, S. (ed.) (2004), *The People's Charter*, London: Merlin.

Saville, J. (1991), *1848: The British State & the Chartist Movement*, Cambridge: CUP.

Thompson, E. P. (1991), *The Making of the English Working Class*, London: Penguin.

Chapter 5

Aris, R. (1998), *Trade Unions and the Management of Industrial Conflict*, London: Macmillan.

Attlee, C. (1937), *The Labour Party in Perspective*, London: Left Book Club.

Britvatti and Hefferman (2000), *The Labour Party, A Centenary History*, London: MacMillan.

Cole, G. D. H. (1948), *The History of the Labour Party*, London: RKP.

Elliott, G. (1993), *Labourism and the English Genius: the Strange Death of Labour England?*, London: Verso.

Kelly, J. (1988), *Trades Unions and Socialist Politics*, London: Verso.

Strachey, J. (1938) *What are We to Do?*, London: Gollancz.

Chapter 6

Campbell, A., Fishman, N. and McIlroy, J. (1999), *British Trade Unions and Industrial Politics*, (2 vols) Ashgate.

Fielding, S.(2003), *The Labour Party*, Palgrave.

Fielding, S., Thompson, P. and Tiratsoo, N. (1945), *The Labour Party And Popular Politics In 1940s Britain*, Manchester: MUP.

Further reading

Francis, M. (1997) *Ideas and Policies Under Labour 1945–1951*, Manchester: MUP.

Fyrth, J. (1995), *Labour's Promised Land*, Lawrence & Wishart.

Hennessey, P. (1994), *Never Again*, Cape.

Morgan, K. O. (1984), *Labour In Power*, Oxford: OUP.

Pearce, R. (1994), *Attlee's Labour Governments 1945-51*, London: Routledge.

Zweiniger-Bargielowska, I. (2002), *Austerity in Britain: Rationing, Controls and Consumption*. Oxford: OUP.

Chapter 7

Liddington, J. and Norris, J. (1978), *One Hand Tied Behind Us: the Rise of the Women's Suffrage Movement*, Virago.

Mitchell, J. (1966), 'Women: The Longest Revolution', in *New Left Review*, 40.

Rowbotham, S. (1973), *Hidden from History: 300 Years of Women's Oppression and the Fight Against It*, various editions.

—— (1997), *A Century of Women: The History of Women in Britain and the United States*, Viking.

Scott, G. (1998), *Feminism and the Politics of Working Women: The Women's Co-operative Guild, 1880s to the Second World War*, UCL Press.

Segal, L. (1997), 'Generations of Feminism', in *Radical Philosophy*, 83 May/June.

Strachey, R. (1928), *The Cause: a Short History of the Women's Movement in Great Britain*, various editions.

Tomalin, C. (1974), *The Life and Death of Mary Wollstonecraft*, various editions.

Chapter 9

Archibugi, D. (ed.) (2003), *Debating Cosmopolitics*, London: Verso.

Dower, N. and Williams, J. (2002), *Global Citizenship: a Reader*, Edinburgh: Edinburgh UP.

Harvey, D. (2005), *A Brief History of Neoliberalism*, Oxford: OUP.

Keane, J. (2003), *Global Civil Society*, Cambridge: CUP.

Todd, M. and Taylor, G. (eds) (2004), *Democracy and Participation: Popular Protest Movements and New Social Movements*, Merlin.

About the contributors

Gill Scott
Gill Scott is Principal Lecturer in the School of Historical and Critical Studies at the University of Brighton. The main focus of her research has been an investigation of the relationship between feminist ideas and the organization of working-class women historically. She has published several articles on the Women's Co-operative Guild, and a book, *Feminism and the Politics of Working Women* (1998). In recent years she has been a member of the 'Gender and Built Space' Research Group in the Faculty of Art and Architecture at the University of Brighton. She has been working on the involvement of the WCG in the development of housing policy in the 1940s, and on the role of the WCG in the suffrage movement prior to the First World War.

William Lamont
William Lamont is Emeritus Professor of History at the University of Sussex. His publications include the biographies of two Puritans, William Prynne and Richard Baxter, and *Last Witnesses; the Muggletonian History, 1652–1979* (2006).

Colin Richmond
Colin Richmond is Emeritus Professor of History at Keele University. His publications include *The Paston Family in the Fifteenth Century* (three volumes); *Campaigner against anti-semitism: the Rev James Parkes (1896–1981)*, and *The Penket Papers*, a volume of short stories.

David Powell
David Powell is a former journalist and film maker, PA-Reuters and

BBC. His publications include *Tom Paine, The Greatest Exile*; *Charles James Fox, Man of the People*; *The Power Game*; *What's Left, Labour Britain and the Socialist Tradition*; and *Tony Benn, a Political Life*.

Paddy Maguire

Paddy Maguire teaches history at the University of Brighton, and is Head of the School of Historical and Critical Studies. He is chair of the History Workshop Trust, and a longstanding member of the Workshop movement as well as having been for a number of years on the Executive of the Society for the Study of Labour History. He has published on the Co-operative movement.

Tom Hickey

Tom Hickey is Principal Lecturer in Philosophy and Politics at the University of Brighton. He teaches Aesthetics, Political Philosophy and Philosophy of Science, and is Course leader of the MA in Cultural and Critical Theory. He is joint convenor of the biennial international conference Globalization and its Discontents. He is currently working on issues of cultural memory, political struggle and artistic representation for an international conference and exhibition in October 2007. He is a member of the NEC of the lecturers union, the UCU.

Tony Benn

An MP for five decades, Tony Benn served first as Postmaster General, and later as Minister of Technology in the first Wilson administration (1964–70), and as Secretary of State for Industry (1974–75). He then served as Secretary of State for Energy (1975–79) in the Wilson, and then the Callaghan governments of the 1970s. His publications include *Arguments for Socialism* (1979), *Arguments for Democracy* (1981), *Common Sense* (1993), and *Dare to be a Daniel* (2004), together with seven volumes of his Diaries.

John Newsinger

John Newsinger is a Senior Lecturer in History at the School of Historical and Cultural Studies, Bath Spa University College. His publications include *Orwell's Politics*; *Rebel City: Larkin, Connolly, and the Dublin Labour Movement*, and most recently, *A People's*

History of the British Empire. John is a member of the Socialist Workers' Party.

John Charlton

John Charlton taught history and politics at Leeds Polytechnic and Leeds University. He has published on coal miners, Chartists, new unions, and resistance to globalization. He is currently working on the origins of sixties radicalism on Tyneside and is involved with the North East Society for Labour History (www.nelh.net).

Index

Acton, Lord 170
Alfred the Great 16
Aristotle 184
Askwith, George 102
Athelred 16
Attlee, Clement 113–14, 120–1, 124–25
Atwood, Thomas 189
Asserian 16

Baldwin, Stanley 105–6, 111
Baxter, Richard 38–9, 41
Beaconsfield, Lord 69
Benn, Tony viii, 3, 5, 44, 188, 193
Bentham, Jeremy 60
Berlin, Isaiah 9
Bethall, Sir Richard 62–3
Bevan, Aneurin 117
Bevin, Ernest 102, 113, 120, 129
Blair, Tony 11, 79–80, 153–4, 156–8, 160, 161, 175, 178
Blunkett, David 183–4
Blunt, Wilfred Scawen 72
Bloc, Marc 24, 33
Bois, Ellen Du 148
Borlese, Edward 41, 43
Boothroyd, Betty 154
Bowring, Sir John 59–61, 63
Bright, John 68, 74–5
Brecht, Bertold 194
Brown, Gordon 175, 178
Buckingham, Duke of 40
Bury, Mrs 138–9
Bush, George W. 11, 153
Burke, Edmund 150
Butler, Colonel William 77

Cade, Jack 31–2

Campbell, Alistair 161
Campbell, J. R. 127–8
Carlyle, Thomas 4
Castlereagh, Viscount 84
Castro, Fidel 46
Carson, Sir Edward 99
Castle, Barbara 119, 128
Chamberlain, Joseph 75–6, 79, 165–6
Charles I 40–1, 44, 46
Churchill, Winston 101, 109
Citrine, Walter 118
Clarke, George 47
Clarke, William 45–8, 49, 54
Clinton, Bill 11
Cobden, Richard 60, 63–9, 74, 166
Con, George 40
Cook, James 107
Cook, Robin 153
Cornewall Lewis, Sir George 63
Cranmer, Thomas 35–6
Cranworth, Lord 63
Cripps, Sir Stafford 111–13, 117, 121, 129
Crossland, Anthony 10
Cromwell, Oliver 2, 6, 96, 44–7, 54
Cromwell, Thomas 35–6

Daines, Percy 115, 118
Dalton, Hugh 112, 114, 117, 125
Darlington, Lord 83
Davies, Emily 136–9, 141–2, 148
Davies, John Llewelyn 136
Davies, Margaret Llewelyn 136
Dilke, Sir Charles 73–5, 80
Douglas, Charles Earl of Argyll 62
Duckham, Sir Arthur 104

Eden, Anthony 78

Index

Edward VIII 156
Elgin, Lord 64, 67

Fairfax, Sir Thomas 44
Firestone, Shulamith 145
Firth, Sir Charles 49–51
Frost, John 91
Forster, E. M. 1
Fukuyama, Francis 168, 171

Gaitskell, Hugh 118, 121, 125
Gallacher, William 127
George C. H. 55
George III 84
George V 110, 113
Gladstone, William 69–77, 79
Goldsmith, Lord 153
Goschen, George 70–1
Gould, Philip 158
Granville, Lord 72–3
Greer, Germaine 145
Grey, Lady Jane 35
Grey, Earl 87, 89

Habermas, Jürgen 187
Hailsham, Lord viii, 150, 151, 152, 162
Haller, William 51–2
Hardie, Keir 98, 101, 111
Harney, Julian 92–4
Harrison, Frederic 76
Heath, Edward 163
Henderson, Arthur 111
Henderson, Frances 47–8, 50, 54
Queen Henrietta Maria 40
Henry VI 32
Henry VIII 35–6
Herbert, Sidney 64
Hitler, Adolf 173
Hodges, Frank 103
Hoffman, Lord 155
Hogg, Quentin 51
Hunt, Henry 82
Hussein, Saddam 79, 153

Ireton, Henry 6, 45–6, 54
Ismail, Khedive 70–1

John, King 18, 19, 21

Jones, Aubrey 119
Jones, Ernest 94
Jordan, W. K. 52

Kelly, David 154
Kennedy, Baroness viii
Keynes, John Maynard 109–10
Kohl, Helmut 10

Laski, Harold 5, 112–13
Laud, Archbishop 40
Lawrence, Susan 106
L'Estrange, Sir Roger 41
Liverpool, Lord 84
Lovett, William 92
Lilburne, John 46
Lindsay, A. D. viii, 50–3
L'Overture, Tousaint 7
Lloyd George, David 99–100, 103–4, 109
Locke, John 48, 53, 162–3, 167
Ludlow, Edmund 41, 43

McDonald, Earl of Antrim 40–1
MacDonald, Ramsey 99–101, 104, 106–8, 110–12, 114
McDouall, Peter Murray 94
MacMillan, Harold 78
Malet, Sir Edward 72
Mandelson, Peter 162
Mann, Thomas 100–1, 104
Maxton, Jimmy 108
Mayhew, Christopher 123
Mill, J. S. 139
Milton, John 48, 151
Mitchell, Juliet 145
Mitterand, François 10
Monck, George 47
More, Thomas 31
Morrice, Roger 50
Morris, William 97–8, 100, 108, 111
Morrison, Herbert 113, 117–18, 120, 122–3, 128
Mosley, Oswald 151
Murdoch, Rupert 161

Nash, Rosalind 139–40

Oates, Titus 43

O'Brien, Bronterre 92–3, 95
O'Connell, Daniel 85
O'Connor, Feargus 90, 92–3
O'Neill, Phelim 40
Orwell, George 2,

Paine, Thomas viii, 3, 5, 42, 168
Palmerstone, Lord 60, 62–4, 79
Pankhurst, Christabel 135
Pankhurst, Emmeline 135
Pankhurst, Sylvia 135
Parkes, Harry 59
Paston, Clement 24
Pease, J. W. 76
de la Pole, William 32
Place, Francis 84
Pottinger, Henry 49
Prescott, John 128
Pym, John 42

Rainborough, Colonel 3, 46, 168
Reddish, Sarah 136–8
Reagan, Ronald 10, 165
Reid, John 179, 183–4
Rhondda, Viscountess 135
Richard, Henry 66, 68
Richard II 27
Richard, Earl of Warwick 32
Richard III 32
Rowbotham, Sheila 134, 146
Robin Hood 25–6
Roosevelt, F. D. 173
Rutherford, Samuel 53
Russell, Bertrand 2, 3, 96, 151
Russell, Conrad 38–9
Russell, Lord John 89, 91

Scott, Lord 155
Samuel, Sir Herbert 111
Sands, Phillipe 154
Schmidt, Karl 183–4
Shaw, G. B. 51, 97, 158

Shelton, Thomas 47
Sidmouth, Viscount 84
Smith, Adam 12, 166
Snowden, Philip 101, 103, 109–10
Sorel, George 100
Spencer, Herbert 76
Strachey, Ray 134
Straw, Jack 178
Stewart, Christopher 180

Tawney, R. H. 5, 53, 113, 152, 163
Thatcher, Margaret 10, 165–166, 171
Thomas, Jimmy 106–107
Thompson, Edward 82, 86
Tillett, Ben 100
Tyler, Wat 27

Urabi, Colonel Ahmed 71, 73, 75

Vincent, Henry 90, 92

Walworth, William 27
Walwyn, William 45, 49
Webb, Beatrice 9, 97, 103, 106–7, 112
Webb, Sidney 9, 97
Wellington, Duke of 86, 87
Whittington, Richard 30
Whitman, Walter 150
Williams, Rowan viii
Williams, Shirley 125
Wilmhurst, Elizabeth 153
Wilson, Harold 121, 124, 125, 128, 157,
    161
Wilson, Rivers 70
Wilson, Woodrow 172
Wildman, John 46
Winstanley, Gerard 54
Wollstonecraft, Mary 132–3
Woodcock, George 119
Wolsey, Cardinal 34
Woodhouse, A. S. P. 50–3, 55
Wycliffe, John 168